THE EPIC O[F]

ODYSSEUS RETUR[NS]

III

XERXES INVADES GREECE HERODOTUS

IV

'THE SEA, THE SEA' XENOPHON

V

THE ABDUCTION OF SITA

VI

JASON AND THE GOLDEN FLEECE APOLLONIUS

VII

EXODUS

VIII

THE DESTRUCTION OF TROY VIRGIL

IX

THE SERPENT'S TEETH OVID

X

THE FALL OF JERUSALEM JOSEPHUS

XI

THE MADNESS OF NERO TACITUS

XII

CUPID AND PSYCHE APULEIUS

XIII

THE LEGENDARY ADVENTURES OF ALEXANDER THE GREAT

XIV

BEOWULF

XV

SIEGFRIED'S MURDER

XVI

SAGAS AND MYTHS OF THE NORTHMEN

XVII

THE SUNJATA STORY

XVIII

THE DESCENT INTO HELL DANTE

XIX

KING ARTHUR'S LAST BATTLE MALORY

XX

THE VOYAGES OF SINDBAD

Josephus

The Fall of Jerusalem

TRANSLATED BY G. A. WILLIAMSON

PENGUIN EPICS

PENGUIN BOOKS

Published by the Penguin Group
Penguin Books Ltd, 80 Strand, London WC2R ORL, England
Penguin Group (USA) Inc., 375 Hudson Street, New York 10014, USA
Penguin Group (Canada), 90 Eglinton Avenue East, Suite 700, Toronto, Ontario, Canada M4P 2Y3
(a division of Pearson Penguin Canada Inc.)
Penguin Ireland, 25 St Stephen's Green, Dublin 2, Ireland (a division of Penguin Books Ltd)
Penguin Group (Australia), 250 Camberwell Road, Camberwell, Victoria 3124, Australia
(a division of Pearson Australia Group Pty Ltd)
Penguin Books India Pvt Ltd, 11 Community Centre, Panchsheel Park, New Delhi – 110 017, India
Penguin Group (NZ), cnr Airborne and Rosedale Roads, Albany,
Auckland 1310, New Zealand (a division of Pearson New Zealand Ltd)
Penguin Books (South Africa) (Pty) Ltd, 24 Sturdee Avenue,
Rosebank, Johannesburg 2196, South Africa

Penguin Books Ltd, Registered Offices: 80 Strand, London WC2R ORL, England

www.penguin.com

This translation of *The Fall of Jerusalem* first published 1959
This extract published in Penguin Books 2006

1

Translation copyright © G. A. Williamson, 1959, 1970
All rights reserved

The moral right of the translator has been asserted

Taken from the Penguin Classics edition of *The Jewish War*
translated by G. A. Williamson

Typeset by Rowland Phototypesetting Ltd, Bury St Edmunds, Suffolk
Printed in England by Clays Ltd, St Ives plc

Except in the United States of America, this book is sold subject
to the condition that it shall not, by way of trade or otherwise, be lent,
re-sold, hired out, or otherwise circulated without the publisher's
prior consent in any form of binding or cover other than that in
which it is published and without a similar condition including this
condition being imposed on the subsequent purchaser

ISBN-13: 978-0-141-02636-7
ISBN-10: 0-141-02636-7

Contents

1. Two Walls Captured — 1
2. The Horrors of the Siege — 26
3. Antonia Captured and Destroyed — 47
4. The Temple Burnt and the City Taken — 75

Note

The Fall of Jerusalem is taken from Josephus' description of *The Jewish War*, the Jewish rebellion against Rome between AD 66 and 70. Originally a rebel, Josephus changed sides after he was captured to become a Rome-appointed negotiator, and so was uniquely placed to observe these turbulent events. *The Fall of Jerusalem* begins with the Romans' brutal blockade of Jerusalem and ends with the horrible, heroic and bloody fall and destruction of the Temple of Masada.

Two Walls Captured

Inside the City the partisan fighters under Simon's command, not counting the Idumaeans, numbered 10,000 under fifty officers, with Simon as commander-in-chief. His Idumaean allies were 5,000 strong, with ten officers, of whom Jacob, son of Sosas, and Simon, son of Cathla, were the accepted leaders. John, after his seizure of the Temple, had 6,000 fully armed men under twenty officers. Later he was joined by the Zealots, who had laid aside their quarrel. These numbered 2,400, led by their old commander Eleazar and Simon, son of Arinus. While these factions, as we said, were fighting each other, the citizens were assailed from two directions at once, and those who would not be accessories to crime were plundered by both parties. Simon held the Upper City and the Great Wall as far as the Kidron, with as much of the Old Wall as bent eastward from Siloam and went down to the palace of Monobazus, king of Adiabene east of Euphrates. He also held the Fountain and part of the Citadel, or Lower City, as far as the castle of Helena, Monobazus' mother. John held the Temple and much of the surrounding area, with Ophel and the Kidron Valley. Everything that lay between them they burnt down to leave room for their fratricidal conflict. For even when the Romans were encamped close to the walls the internal strife continued to rage. At the time of

The Fall of Jerusalem

the first sortie they had momentarily recovered their wits; but their frenzy had quickly returned, co-operation was at an end, and the internal struggle was resumed as if their one desire was to play into the hands of the besiegers. They suffered nothing worse at Roman hands than they had endured at each other's, and when they had finished there was nothing new left for the City to undergo – she went through greater agony before she fell, and her destroyers accomplished something greater. I mean that her internal divisions destroyed the City, and the Romans destroyed the internal divisions, which were far more firmly established than her walls; and the misery of it all could reasonably be put down to her own people, the justice of it to the Romans. But everyone must interpret the facts in his own way.

Such being the state of affairs within the City, Titus with some picked horsemen rode round outside, looking for the best point for an assault on the walls. Seeing no hope anywhere else, as where the valleys ran there was no access and elsewhere the first wall seemed too solid for his engines, he decided to deliver his assault near the tomb of John the high priest; for there the first rampart was lower and the second was not joined to it, little trouble having been taken with the fortifications where the New City was thinly populated, while it was easy to approach the third through which he planned to invade the Upper City, force his way through Antonia, and capture the Temple. While he was riding round an arrow struck one of his staff, Nicanor, in the left shoulder, as a result of his approaching too near with Josephus in an endeavour to put peace proposals before the sentries

Two Walls Captured

on the walls, who knew him well. This brought home to Caesar their determination, for they would not leave unmolested even those who came near to save them: it spurred him on to begin the siege, and he at once gave his infantry leave to devastate the suburbs, and ordered timber to be collected and platforms constructed. Dividing his army into three sections for this work, he stationed the spearmen and bowmen between the platforms and in front of these the spear-throwers, catapults, and stone-throwers, to prevent any enemy sorties directed against the works and any attempted interference from the wall. The felling of the trees at once stripped the suburbs bare, but the collection of the timber for the platforms and the concentration of the whole army on the work were accompanied by feverish activity on the Jewish side. Consequently the citizens who had been at the mercy of robbers and cut-throats now recovered their spirits, confident that they would have a breathing-space while the enemy without kept their persecutors busy, and that they would be revenged on them if the Romans were victorious.

John, however, though his men were eager to attack the Romans, was immobilized by fear of Simon. Simon on the other hand was active enough, being nearer to the besiegers. He mounted his artillery along the wall, the weapons taken from Cestius earlier on and those captured when they overwhelmed the defenders of Antonia. These, however, most of the men were unable to use owing to inexperience, but following instruction from deserters a few managed to use their engines after a fashion, besides showering stones and arrows on the builders from the wall and dashing out in company strength to engage them hand to hand. The workmen were shielded from the missiles by wicker screens laid across palisades, while the artillery halted the sorties. The engines of all the legions were masterpieces of construction, but none were equal to those of the Tenth; their spear-throwers were more powerful and their stone-throwers bigger, so that they could repulse not only the sorties but also the fighters on the wall. The stone missiles weighed half a hundredweight and travelled four hundred yards or more; no one who got in their way, whether in the front line or far behind, remained standing. At first the Jews kept watch for the stone – it was white, so that not only was it heard whizzing through the air but its shining surface could easily be seen. Look-outs posted on the towers gave them warning every time a stone was shot from the engine and came hurtling towards them, by shouting 'Baby on the way!' Those in its path at once scattered and fell prone, a precaution which resulted in the stone's passing harmlessly through till it came to a stop. The Roman counter was to blacken the stone. As it could not then be seen so easily, they hit their target, destroying many with a single shot. But in spite of their casualties the Jews did not allow the Romans to raise their platforms in safety; every device of inventiveness and daring was called into play as they fought night and day to keep them out.

When the works were finished the engineers measured the distance to the wall by throwing lead and line from the platforms: no other way was possible under the barrage from above. When they found that the

Two Walls Captured

battering-rams could reach it, they brought them up. Titus next posted his artillery nearer to prevent the Jews from keeping the rams away, and ordered the battering to begin. From three sides a frightful din suddenly resounded round the City, a shout went up from those within and the partisans were as terrified as the rest. Both parties seeing the common danger realized at last that they must make a common defence. The rivals shouted across to each other that they were giving the enemy every possible assistance, when the right thing, even if God did not give them permanent concord, was for the moment at any rate to set aside their mutual animosities and unite against the Romans. Simon then announced that everyone was free to proceed from the Temple to the wall, and John gave his permission though suspicious of Simon. Hatred and private differences utterly forgotten, they became one body, and manning the wall they flung firebrands by the hundred against the engines, and showered weapons continuously on the men shoving the battering-rams. The bolder spirits sprang forward in tight groups, tore to pieces the screens over the engines, and falling on the crews overpowered them, not so much by skill as by reckless courage. Titus himself never failed to come to the help of those in difficulty; he placed the cavalry and bowmen on either side of the engines, beat off the fire-throwers, repulsed those who were hurling missiles from the towers, and got the battering-rams into action. Yet the wall did not give way under the blows, except that the Fifteenth Legion's ram knocked away the corner of a tower. The wall itself was undamaged: it was not in the same

The Fall of Jerusalem

immediate danger as the tower, which projected a long way and could not easily involve the collapse of any part of the actual rampart.

Suspending their sorties for a while the Jews kept watch on the Romans, who had scattered to their tasks and about the camps under the impression that the defenders had withdrawn through exhaustion and terror. Suddenly they poured out en masse by a hidden gate near the tower Hippicus, armed with brands to set fire to the works and bent on reaching the Roman fortifications. At their shouts the front-line troops manned their posts and the supports came running up. But the reckless courage of the Jews was too quick for the solid defence of the Romans: they routed their foremost opponents and swept on to attack the reserves. A furious battle was joined round the engines, one side straining every nerve to set them on fire, the other to prevent it: a babel of sounds arose from both and many of those in the forefront were killed. The Jews were gaining the advantage through sheer desperation, the works were catching fire and would probably have been completely destroyed, engines and all, had not the picked troops from Alexandria with few exceptions stood fast, surpassing their own reputation for gallantry; for in this battle they put more famous legions in the shade. At last Caesar brought up the flower of his cavalry and charged the enemy. Twelve of the leading Jews he killed with his right hand. Their fate broke the resistance of the rest: Titus followed, drove them in a body into the City, and saved the works from the flames. It happened that in this battle one of the Jews was taken alive. Titus ordered him to be crucified before the walls, hoping that the sight would terrify the rest into surrender. After the withdrawal John, the Idumaean leader, was talking to a soldier of his acquaintance before the wall when he was struck in the breast by an Arab arrow and died instantly – a terrible shock to the Idumaeans and a grief to the insurgents; for his prowess and ability were both outstanding.

The next night the Romans were thrown into confusion by a surprising occurrence. Titus had ordered the construction of three towers 75 feet high, to be set up on three platforms so that from them he might bombard the defenders on the wall. But in the middle of the night one of these fell down spontaneously with a tremendous crash, causing panic in the army. Convinced that an attack was imminent all rushed for their weapons, and wild confusion seized the legions. As no one could say what had occurred, they scattered in all directions with cries of anguish, and when no enemy appeared they grew scared of each other, and everyone anxiously asked his neighbour for the password as if the Jews had broken into their camps. They were like men in the grip of panic fear, till, learning what had occurred, Titus ordered it to be explained to them all, and at long last they recovered from their confusion.

The Jews stood up obstinately to every other form of attack but were in great difficulty from the towers. From them they were pelted by the lighter engines and by the spearmen, bowmen and stone-throwers. On their lofty perch these men were beyond the reach of Jewish weapons, and there was no way to capture the towers, which were difficult to overturn because of their weight and could not be set alight because of the iron that encased them. So they withdrew out of range, abandoning the attempt to hold off the assaults of the Romans, which by their incessant blows were little by little effecting their purpose. Already the wall was giving way before Victor (so the Jews nicknamed the biggest Roman battering-ram, as being victorious over everything) and they had long been worn out by fighting and sentry-go and night-duty far from the City. Besides, through laziness and their habit of deciding wrongly, they thought it a waste of effort to defend this wall as there remained two more behind it. Most of them slacked off and retired; and when the Romans climbed through the breach made by Victor, they all left their posts and ran helter-skelter to the second wall. Those who had broken through then opened the gates and let in the whole army. Having thus mastered the first wall on the fifteenth day of the siege, the 7th of Artemisios, the Romans demolished a large part of it, together with the northern suburbs of the City, so recently destroyed by Cestius.

Titus now accommodated his troops within the first wall in the traditional Camp of the Assyrians, occupying all the intervening ground as far as the Kidron, but out of bowshot from the second wall, and at once began probing attacks. Dividing their forces the Jews kept up an obstinate defence from the wall, John's men fighting from Antonia and the northern colonnade of the Temple and before the tomb of King Alexander, Simon's brigade occupying the approach near the tomb of John the high priest and defending the ground as far as the gate by

Two Walls Captured

which water was brought in to the Hippicus Tower. Over and over again they sprang out from the gates and fought at close quarters; and though chased back to the wall and worsted in these hand-to-hand struggles, being far less skilled than the Romans, they scored in the wall-fighting. The Romans were upheld by the combination of strength with experience, the Jews by reckless courage nourished by fear, and by their characteristic obstinacy amid disasters; and they still had hopes of survival, as the Romans had of a quick victory. Neither side showed any sign of flagging: assaults, wall-fighting, sorties at company strength went on continuously all day long: no method of attack was left untried. Dusk hardly availed to break off the battles begun at dawn, and there was no sleep for either side – indeed the night was less endurable than the day, the Jews expecting every moment the capture of the wall, the Romans an assault on their camps. Both passed the night in arms; yet the first glimmer of dawn found them ready for battle.

Among the Jews the great ambition was to show outstanding courage and earn the gratitude of their officers. Simon was held in special respect and awe, and so devoted to him was every man under his command that none would have hesitated a moment to kill himself at Simon's bidding. With the Romans, the great inducements to valour were the habit of victory and unfamiliarity with defeat, their constant campaigning and uninterrupted training, and the greatness of the Empire – above all the fact that always, in every place, by every man stood Titus. To show weakness when

Caesar was there fighting at their side was unthinkable, while the man who fought valiantly did so before the eyes of the one who would reward him; indeed, he was paid already if Caesar had recognized his courage. As a result many showed courage beyond their strength through sheer enthusiasm. Here is an instance. On one of those days the Jews were drawn up before the wall in force, and the opposing lines were still exchanging spears at long range. Suddenly Longinus, a cavalryman, leapt out of the Roman ranks and charged the very middle of the Jewish phalanx. Scattering them by his onslaught he killed two of the most stalwart, striking one in the face as he came to meet him, withdrawing the spear and transfixing the other through the side as he turned away. Then back from the middle of the enemy he ran to his own lines unscathed. When he had given this demonstration of prowess, there were many who imitated his valour. The Jews on their side, heedless of the damage they suffered, were concerned only with what they could inflict, and death had no terrors for them if only it fell on one of the enemy too. But Titus was as anxious for the safety of his men as for victory itself. He declared that incautious enthusiasm was utter madness, and heroism was heroic only when it went with prudent regard for the hero's own safety. His men were forbidden to risk their own lives in order to display their fearlessness.

He now brought up the battering-ram against the middle tower of the north wall. There a cunning Jew named Castor lay in ambush with ten others like himself, the rest having withdrawn to escape the arrows. These for a time kept quiet, crouching behind the parapet, but

Two Walls Captured

when the tower began to disintegrate they stood up and Castor, holding out his hands as if in supplication, called on Caesar and in heart-rending tones besought him to pity them. Guileless himself, Titus believed him, and hoping that the Jews had at last come to their senses, stopped the blows of the ram, allowed no arrows to be aimed at the supplicants, and invited Castor to state his wishes. When he replied that he would like to come down under a guarantee of impunity, Titus expressed delight at his good sense; he would be still more delighted if everyone felt the same, and gladly gave the City his word. Of the ten men five pretended to join in Castor's supplication, but the rest loudly protested that they would never be slaves of the Romans while they could die as free men. During the long wrangle that followed the assault was held up, and Castor sent to Simon bidding him take his time in deciding the necessary steps, as he could delude the Roman command indefinitely. At the same time as he sent this message he made it appear that he was urging the objectors to accept the guarantee. They made a show of indignation, brandishing their naked swords above the parapet, then struck their own breastplates and fell down as if run through. Titus and his staff were dumbfounded at the extraordinary courage of the men, and being unable to see from below just what had happened admired their fortitude and pitied their misfortune.

At this point someone shot an arrow and hit Castor at the side of his nose. He at once drew it out and showed it to Titus, complaining of unfair treatment. Reprimanding the archer Caesar deputed Josephus, who was standing by, to convey the guarantee to Castor and shake hands on it. But Josephus refused to go himself, since the petitioners meant no good, and restrained those of his friends who were anxious to take his place. However Aeneas, one of the deserters, said he would go, and when Castor called for someone to receive the money that he had with him, Aeneas spread out his garments to catch it and ran towards him more eagerly. Castor promptly picked up a huge stone and flung it at him. Aeneas dodged out of the way, but it injured another soldier who had come forward. When Caesar saw how he had been tricked, he realized that it was fatal to show pity in war: sterner measures gave the trickster less opportunity. Furious that he had been fooled, he stepped up the assaults of the battering-ram. As the tower was on the point of collapse, Castor and his men set fire to it, and then leapt through the blaze into the vault beneath, thus again giving the Romans an impression of bravery by apparently flinging themselves into the fire.

Caesar captured the wall at this point four days after capturing the first, and as the Jews had retired from it he entered with 1,000 heavy infantry and his special bodyguard, in that part of the New City where the wool-shops, forges, and cloth-market were, and the streets ran slantwise to the wall. If he had without hesitation demolished a longer stretch of the wall, or after entering had by right of conquest sacked what he had taken, his victory would not, I think, have been cancelled out by a reverse. As it was, hoping to shame the Jews by waiving his right to do them hurt, he

Two Walls Captured

refrained from widening the breach to ensure an easy retreat: he never imagined they would repay his kindness with treachery. So after his entry he forbade his men to kill any prisoners or set the houses on fire; the partisans he informed that, if they wished to fight without harming the citizens, they were free to march out; to the citizens he promised the return of their property. For his chief concern was to preserve the City for himself and the Temple for the City.

The people had been ready from the first to accept his demands, but the war-party took humanity for weakness and imagined that it was through inability to take the rest of the City that Titus made these offers. Threatening the townsfolk with death if there was any suggestion of surrender, and murdering all who mentioned the word 'peace', they attacked the Romans inside the wall, some pouncing on them in the narrow streets or from the houses, while others made a dash outside the wall from the upper gates. In hopeless confusion the guards on the wall jumped down from the towers and withdrew to their camps. A clamour arose from those within, completely encircled by the enemy, and from those without, in fear for those left behind. The Jews, every minute more numerous, and at a great advantage through familiarity with the streets, wounded many and by relentless pressure forced them towards the exit. They, having no other choice, continued to resist; for it was impossible to escape in a body through the narrow gap in the wall. It is probable that all who had entered the City would have been cut to pieces had not Titus come to the rescue. Placing his bowmen at the ends of the streets and taking

The Fall of Jerusalem

his own stand where the enemy were thickest, he stopped their advance with his arrows, aided by Domitius Sabinus, who in this battle again showed his worth. Firm as a rock, Caesar kept up a constant stream of arrows and pinned down the Jews till all his men had got clear.

Thus the Romans after capturing the second wall were driven out again. The war-party in Jerusalem were elated, carried away by their success, and convinced that if the Romans ever did venture to set foot in the City again they were doomed to defeat. For God was blinding their eyes because of their transgressions, and they saw neither the strength of the remaining Roman forces – so much more numerous than those they had ejected – nor the famine that was creeping towards them. It was still possible to feed on the public miseries and drink the City's life-blood, though want had long been assailing honest men and for lack of necessities many were at death's door. But the partisans welcomed the destruction of the people: it left more for them. The only people who, in their opinion, deserved to survive were those who had no use for peace and only lived to defeat the Romans: the masses who opposed them were a mere drag, and they were glad to see them go. Such was their attitude to those within the walls; and when the Romans again tried to break in, they held them up by filling the breach and walling it up with their bodies. For three days they stood their ground, resisting with the utmost determination; but on the fourth Titus delivered a violent onslaught which overcame their defence and forced them to retire as before. Once more in possession of the wall, he at once threw down the northern stretch from

Two Walls Captured

end to end, and placing garrisons in the towers on the portion towards the south began to plan the assault on the third wall.

He now resolved to suspend the siege for a time and so afford the partisans an interval for deliberation, in the hope that they would be inclined to surrender in view of the demolition of the second wall or through fear of starvation; for plunder would not keep them going for long. This interval he turned to his own advantage as follows. When the soldiers' pay-day arrived, he ordered the officers to parade their troops in full view of the enemy and there count out the money to each man. In accordance with custom the soldiers removed their armour from its protective coverings and advanced in full panoply, the horsemen leading their chargers decked in all their trappings. Every yard of ground before the City shone with silver and gold, a spectacle that filled the Romans with delight, their enemies with terror. Spectators crowded the whole length of the Old Wall and the north side of the Temple, and behind the wall eyes could be seen peering from every window – nowhere in the City was there an inch of ground not hidden by the crowds. Utter consternation seized even the boldest when they saw the entire army assembled, the splendour of their armour and the perfect discipline of the men. I have little doubt that at this sight the partisans would have abandoned their stand, had not the limitless mischief they had done to the citizens destroyed all hope of pardon by the Romans. Death by torture awaited them if they turned back now: death in battle was greatly to be preferred. Fate, too, ordained that with the guilty should perish the innocent, and with the warring factions the entire City.

In four days the Romans completed the payment of all the legions. On the fifth, as no request for peace came from the Jews, Titus divided his legions into two groups and began building platforms in front of Antonia and the Tomb of John, planning to invade the Upper City at the Tomb and the Temple via Antonia: if the Temple was not taken, not even possession of the town would be secure. At each of these points work on two platforms was begun, every legion being responsible for one. The men working alongside the Tomb were hindered by the Idumaeans and Simon's infantry, who made surprise sorties; those before Antonia by John's men and the Zealot groups. These attackers had the advantage not only because they were hurling their missiles from a greater height, but also because they had now learnt to use their engines; for daily practice had steadily increased their skill. They had three hundred spear-throwers and forty stone-throwers, enabling them to make work on the Roman platforms difficult. Titus knew that the survival or destruction of the City mattered very much to himself; so while he prosecuted the siege he did not fail to urge the Jews to reverse their policy, combining military activity with good advice. Knowing too that very often the sword is less effective than the tongue, he called on them repeatedly to save themselves by handing over the City, virtually his already, and sent Josephus to talk to them in their own language, thinking they would perhaps yield to the persuasions of a fellow-countryman.

Josephus circled the wall, striving to keep out of range

but within hearing, and appealing to them again and again to spare themselves and their people, their country and their Temple, and not to show themselves more indifferent than were foreigners. The Romans, who had no share in them, respected their enemies' holy places and till now had kept their hands off them, while those who had been brought up in them, and if they survived would alone possess them, were doing their best to destroy them. Did they not see their strongest walls lying flat, and only the weakest one still standing? Did they not know that the might of Rome was invincible, and submission to her an everyday experience? If it indeed was right to fight for freedom, they should have done so at the start; once they had been crushed, and had submitted for many years, to try then to shake off the yoke was to show, not a love of freedom, but a morbid desire for death. It might well be reasonable to disdain meaner masters, but not the lords of the whole world. What corner of the earth had escaped the Romans, unless heat or cold made it of no value to them? From every side fortune had passed to them, and God, who handed dominion over from nation to nation round the world, abode now in Italy. It was an immutable and unchallenged law among beasts and men alike, that all must submit to the stronger, and that power belonged to those supreme in arms. That was why their ancestors, in soul and body and in resources far superior to themselves, had submitted to Rome – which they could not have borne to do if they had not known that God was on the Roman side.

As for themselves, what gave them confidence to hold

out, when most of the City was already captured and those inside, even if the walls were still standing, were worse off than if the City had fallen? The Romans were well aware of the famine within, which was now destroying the civilian population and would soon destroy the fighting-men as well. Even if the Romans suspended operations and made no armed assault on the City, yet a war there was no resisting was raging in their midst and growing every hour – unless they could take arms and fight against famine itself, and alone among men master even hunger! They had better change their ways, he went on, before it was too late, and veer to a safer course while they could: the Romans would bear them no grudge for their past folly unless they brazened it out to the end: they were by nature merciful in victory, and they never allowed bitter feelings to stand in the way of their interests, which would not be served by having the City uninhabited or the country desolate. And so Caesar was ready even now to offer them guarantees; but he would not spare a single man if he took the City by storm, least of all if even at their last gasp they turned down his offers. That the third wall would be quickly captured was evident from the capture of the other two: even if that barrier defied attack, hunger would fight for the Romans and against them.

These appeals of Josephus were received by the defenders generally with howls of derision or execration, sometimes with showers of stones. As frank advice was lost on them, he turned to the story of the nation's past.

'You wretched people!' he cried, 'you forget your real allies. Are you fighting the Romans with weapons and

Two Walls Captured

your own right hand? Whom else have we defeated in that way? and when did God our Creator fail to avenge our wrongs? Turn round and look at the place you are setting out from to the fight, and think how powerful an Ally you have grossly insulted! Have you forgotten the miraculous achievements of your fathers, and the terrible wars this place has won for you in days gone by? For my part, I shudder to recall the works of God in your unworthy hearing – listen all the same, and realize that you are fighting not only the Romans but God as well.

'Pharaoh Necho, king of Egypt at the time, descended on this land with an immense army and seized Sarah the Princess, mother of our nation. And what did her husband, our forefather Abraham, do? Did he avenge the insult by force of arms? Yet he had three hundred and eighteen officers under him, with unlimited manpower at their disposal! Did he not regard them as valueless without the help of God, and stretch out clean hands towards the place you now have desecrated, enlisting the Almighty as his Helper? Wasn't the queen sent back to her husband the very next evening, unsullied, while the Egyptian, reverencing the place stained by you with your country-men's blood and shaken by terrible dreams in the night, fled, showering silver and gold on God's beloved Hebrews?

'Need I speak of our fathers' sojourn in Egypt? They were crushed and subject to foreign rulers for four hundred years; but though they might have resisted with weapons and their own right hand, they committed their cause to God. Who has not heard of Egypt, overrun with every wild beast and wasted by every disease, the barren land, the shrunken Nile, the ten plagues in swift succession, and the consequent departure of our fathers, sent on their way with no bloodshed and no danger, led forth by God to establish His temple-worship? Again, when the Syrians carried off our sacred Ark, did not Philistia and Dagon the idol, did not the whole nation of plunderers rue the day? Their hidden parts suppurating, their bowels prolapsed, they brought it back with the hands that stole it, propitiating the Sanctuary with the sound of cymbals and timbrels and with peace-offerings of every kind. It was God whose generalship won this victory for our fathers, because they placed no trust in their right arm or their weapons but committed to Him the decision of the issue.

'When the king of Assyria, Sennacherib, brought all Asia with him and encamped round this City, did he fall by human hands? Wasn't it when those hands were unarmed and raised in supplication that an angel of God in one night destroyed that innumerable army, so that when he arose in the early morning the Assyrian found 185,000 corpses, and fled with the survivors from unarmed Hebrews who attempted no pursuit? You know too of the bondage in Babylon, where the people lived in exile for seventy years, and never tried to shake off the yoke till Cyrus granted them liberty as an offering to God. They were sent on their way by him to re-establish the temple-worship of their Ally.

'In short, on no occasion did our fathers succeed by force of arms, or fail without them after committing their cause to God. If they took no action, they were victorious as it seemed good to their Judge: if they gave battle, they were beaten every time. For instance, when the king of Babylon was besieging this city, and our king Zedekiah disregarding Jeremiah's prophecies gave battle, he was taken prisoner himself and saw the town and the Temple razed to the ground. Yet how moderate that king was compared with your leaders, and his subjects compared with you! Jeremiah shouted from the housetops that they were hated by God for their iniquities against Him, and would be taken into captivity unless they surrendered the City; yet neither king nor people put him to death. But you! I will say nothing of happenings in the City – I have no words to describe the atrocities you have perpetrated; but when I appeal to you to save yourselves you greet me with howls of execration and showers of stones, enraged at being reminded of your sins and unable to endure any mention of the outrages you openly commit day after day!

'Again, when Antiochus Epiphanes was blockading the City and had committed gross sacrilege, and our ancestors advanced in arms against him, what happened? They were cut to pieces in the battle, the town was plundered by the enemy, and the Sanctuary was desolated for three years and a half. Need I go on with the story? But who enlisted the Romans against our country? Wasn't the impiety of the inhabitants responsible? And what began our servitude? Wasn't it civil strife among our ancestors, when the insane rivalry of Aristobulus and Hyrcanus brought Pompey against the City and God put beneath the Roman heel those who did not deserve to be free? After three months' siege they surrendered, though they had not sinned against the Sanctuary and the Law as you have done – and were far better equipped for war. And we know the end of Antigonus, the son of Aristobulus, don't we? In his reign God by a further capture of the City smote the people for their iniquities: Herod, Antipater's heir, brought Sosius, and Sosius a Roman army, which blockaded and besieged them for six months, till as the punishment of their sins they saw the City captured and plundered by their enemies.

'Thus it was never intended that our nation should bear arms, and war has invariably ended in defeat. It is the duty, I believe, of those who dwell on holy ground to commit all things to the judgement of God, and to scorn the aid of human hands whenever they can reach the ear of the heavenly Judge. But which of the things blessed by the lawgiver have *you* done? Which of the things cursed by him have you left undone? How far those who were defeated in earlier days fell short of your impiety! You have not eschewed the secret sins – theft, treachery, adultery; in plundering and murder you vie with each other; you open up new avenues of vice. The Temple has become a sink for the nation's dregs, and native hands have polluted the hallowed spot that even Romans venerated from a distance, setting aside many of their own customs from regard for your Law.

'After all this do you expect Him you have dishonoured to be your ally? You are indeed righteous suppliants and it is with clean hands that you beseech your Helper! With such hands no doubt our king made supplications for aid against the Assyrian, when in one night that mighty army was struck down by God! Are the Romans behaving so like the Assyrian that you can expect a like vengeance on them? Isn't the truth that whereas he received money from our king on the understanding that he would not sack the City, and then descended on us, in defiance of his oaths, to burn the Sanctuary, the Romans are only demanding the customary tribute which our fathers paid to theirs? When they obtain this, they will neither sack the City nor lay a finger on your holy places: they will give you everything else, the freedom of your children, the security of your property, and the preservation of your holy Law. It is madness to expect God to treat the just as He treated the unjust!

'Again, He knows how to take immediate vengeance when there is need; thus on the very night the Assyrians pitched their camp by the City He crushed them. So if He had judged our generation worthy of liberty or the Romans of chastisement, He would immediately have fallen upon them as He fell upon the Assyrians. When? – when Pompey meddled with our affairs, when later Sosius came against us, when Vespasian was laying Galilee waste, and last of all now when Titus was drawing near the City. And yet Magnus and Sosius not only suffered no setback but took the City by assault, and Vespasian made his war against us the stepping-stone to the throne, while for Titus the very springs flow more abundantly, springs that had dried up for you! Before his advent you know that Siloam was falling, as were all the springs outside the town, so that water had to be bought by the pailful; but now they are in such full flood for your enemies that there is more than enough not only for them and their beasts but even for gardens. The same portent you saw happen once before at the capture of the City, when the Babylonian already referred to marched against it, took the City and Sanctuary and burnt them both, though that generation was surely guilty of no such impiety as yours. So I am sure the Almighty has quitted your holy places and stands now on the side of your enemies. Why, when a good man will quit a licentious house and abominate its occupants, do you think God can endure the wickedness of His household – God, who sees each hidden thing and hears what is wrapped in silence? But what do you wrap in silence or keep hidden? What have you not paraded before your enemies? You boast of your unspeakable crimes and daily vie with one another to see who can be the worst, as proud of your vices as if they were virtues!

'In spite of all, a way of salvation still remains if you will follow it, and the Almighty is ready to pardon those who confess and repent. You obdurate fools! throw away your weapons, take pity on your birthplace at this moment plunging to ruin, turn round and gaze at the beauty of what you are betraying – what a City! what a Temple! what gifts from all the Gentile world! Against these will any man direct the flames? Does any man wish these things to pass away? What better deserves to be kept safe than these, you inhuman, stony-hearted monsters! If the sight of these things leaves you unmoved, at least pity your families, and let each man set before his eyes his wife and children and parents, so soon to perish by famine or the sword. I know that danger threatens my own mother and wife, a family of great promise and a house famous from of old; and perhaps you think it is for their sake I advise you. Kill them! take my flesh and blood as the price of your own salvation! I too am ready to die, if that will teach you wisdom.'

The Horrors of the Siege

Tears ran down Josephus' face as he concluded his vehement appeal. The partisans would not give way as they thought a change of front would be disastrous, but among the common people there was a movement in favour of desertion. Some sold all their property at a dead loss, others parted with the more valuable of their treasures. Then to frustrate the bandits they swallowed their gold pieces, and deserting to the Romans had only to empty their bowels to have ample provision for their needs. For most of them were allowed by Titus to go through into the countryside in any direction they chose. This made them still more ready to desert, as they would thus escape from the horrors within the City without being enslaved by the Romans. The supporters of John and Simon made greater efforts to keep these men in than to keep the Romans out, and anyone who afforded even a shadow of suspicion was promptly put to death.

For the wealthy it was just as dangerous to stay in the City as to leave it; for on the pretext that he was a deserter many a man was killed for the sake of his money. As the famine grew worse, the frenzy of the partisans increased with it, and every day these two terrors strengthened their grip. For as corn was nowhere to be seen, men broke into the houses and ransacked them. If

The Horrors of the Siege

they found any, they maltreated the occupants for saying there was none; if they did not, they suspected them of having hidden it more carefully and tortured them. Proof of whether or not they had food was provided by the appearance of the unhappy wretches. If they still had flesh on their bones, they were deemed to have plenty of stores; if they were already reduced to skeletons, they were passed over, for it seemed pointless to dispatch those who were certain to die of starvation before long. Many secretly exchanged their possessions for one measure of corn – wheat if they happened to be rich, barley if they were poor. Then they shut themselves up in the darkest corners of their houses, where some through extreme hunger ate their grain as it was, others made bread, necessity and fear being the only guides. Nowhere was a table laid – they snatched the food from the fire while still uncooked and ate like wolves.

The sight of such misery would have brought tears to the eyes, for while the strong had more than enough, the weak were in desperate straits. All human feelings, alas, yield to hunger, of which decency is always the first victim; for when hunger reigns, restraint is abandoned. Thus it was that wives robbed their husbands, children their fathers, and – most horrible of all – mothers their babies, snatching the food out of their very mouths; and when their dearest ones were dying in their arms, they did not hesitate to deprive them of the morsels that might have kept them alive. This way of satisfying their hunger did not go unnoticed: everywhere the partisans were ready to swoop even on such pickings. Wherever they saw a locked door they concluded that those within were having a meal, and instantly bursting the door open they rushed in, and hardly stopped short at squeezing their throats to force out the morsels of food! They beat old men who held on to their crusts, and tore the hair of women who hid what was in their hands. They showed no pity for grey hairs or helpless infancy, but picked up the children as they clung to their precious scraps and dashed them on the floor. If anyone anticipated their entry by gulping down what they hoped to seize, they felt themselves defrauded and retaliated with worse savagery still.

Terrible were the methods of torture they devised in their quest for food. They stuffed bitter vetch up the genital passages of their victims, and drove sharp stakes into their seats. Torments horrible even to hear about they inflicted on people to make them admit possession of one loaf or reveal the hiding-place of a single handful of barley. It was not that the tormentors were hungry – their actions would have been less barbarous had they sprung from necessity – but rather they were keeping their passions exercised and laying in stores for use in the coming days. Again, when men had crawled out in the night as far as the Roman guardposts to collect wild plants and herbs, these marauders met them just when they thought they had got safely away from the enemy lines and snatched their treasures from them. Piteous entreaties and appeals to the awful Name of God could not secure the return of even a fraction of what they had collected at such risk: they were lucky to be only robbed and not killed as well.

While the humbler folk suffered thus at the hands

The Horrors of the Siege

of mere henchmen, men of position or wealth were dragged before the party chiefs. Some of them were falsely accused of plotting and destroyed, others were charged with betraying the City to the Romans; but the favourite device was to pay an informer to allege that they were planning to desert. When a man had been stripped by Simon he was sent to John: when someone had been plundered by John, Simon took him over. They drank each other's health in the blood of their countrymen and divided the carcases of the wretches between them. In their desire for domination the two were at daggers drawn, but in their crimes they were blood-brothers; for the one who did not give his partner a share in the fruits of other people's misery was deemed an utter scoundrel, while the one who received no share, as if robbed of a prize, was furious at being excluded from the savagery. To give a detailed account of their outrageous conduct is impossible, but we may sum it up by saying that no other city has ever endured such horrors, and no generation in history has fathered such wickedness. In the end they brought the whole Hebrew race into contempt in order to make their own impiety seem less outrageous in foreign eyes, and confessed the painful truth that they were slaves, the dregs of humanity, bastards, and outcasts of their nation. The overthrow of the City was their work, though they forced the unwilling Romans to be credited with a melancholy victory, and almost hurried the flames to the Sanctuary as if they were too slow! It is certain that as they watched it burning from the Upper City, they did not turn a hair or shed a tear, though the Romans were deeply moved.

The Fall of Jerusalem

But of this I shall speak later at the proper time, giving a full account of the circumstances.

On the Roman side the platforms were nearing completion, though the defenders' missiles caused many casualties among the soldiers. Titus himself detailed a section of the cavalry to ambush those who sallied out along the valleys in search of food. Some of these were fighting-men no longer satisfied with what they could steal, but the majority were penniless workers, afraid to desert lest their families should be penalized; for they knew the partisans would catch them if they tried to get their wives and children through the lines, and they could not bear to leave them behind for the bandits to murder in their stead. But hunger gave them courage for these sallies, the only thing left being to slip out and fall into enemy hands. When caught they were forced to offer resistance, and when the fighting ended it seemed too late to sue for mercy. Scourged and subjected before death to every torture, they were finally crucified in view of the wall. Titus indeed realized the horror of what was happening, for every day five hundred – sometimes even more – fell into his hands. However it was not safe to let men captured by force go free, and to guard such a host of prisoners would tie up a great proportion of his troops. But his chief reason for not stopping the slaughter was the hope that the sight of it would perhaps induce the Jews to surrender in order to avoid the same fate. The soldiers themselves through rage and bitterness nailed up their victims in various attitudes as a grim joke, till owing to the vast numbers there was no room for the crosses, and no crosses for the bodies.

The Horrors of the Siege

So far were the partisans from changing their policy in view of this calamity that they went to the opposite extreme in tricking the rest of the people. They dragged the families of the deserters on to the wall with those members of the public who were ready to accept Roman assurances, and showed them what happened to men who deserted to the enemy, declaring that the victims were suppliants, not prisoners. This caused many who were eager to desert to remain in the City, until the truth came out; but some crossed over without further delay, knowing the fate that awaited them but regarding death at enemy hands as a deliverance, compared with starvation. Many of these prisoners Titus ordered to have their hands cut off, that they might not be thought to have deserted and might be believed because of their horrible treatment. Then he sent them to Simon and John, urging these two to put an immediate end to their resistance and not compel him to destroy the City, but to reap the benefit of a change of heart, belated as it was, and save their own lives, their wonderful birthplace, and the Sanctuary that was theirs alone. At the same time he went from platform to platform urging on the workers, to show that he would shortly follow up words with deed. In answer the men on the wall hurled insults at Caesar himself and at his father, and shouted that they cared nothing for death, but preferred it to slavery, as men should. They would do all possible damage to the Romans while they had breath in them. What did their birthplace matter to those who, as he himself said, were doomed to die? As for the Sanctuary, God had a better one in the world itself; but this one too would be saved by Him who dwelt in it, and having Him on their side they would laugh at every threat not backed by deeds; for the issue lay with God. Such were the retorts which they yelled, along with mere abuse.

At this time Antiochus Epiphanes arrived with a large force of heavy infantry and a bodyguard of so-called Macedonians, all just out of their teens, tall, and trained and equipped in the Macedonian manner – hence the title, though few of them bore much resemblance to that martial race! As it happened, the most prosperous of Rome's vassals was the king of Commagene – until his luck changed. In his old age he declared that no man should be called happy before his death. But Antiochus, who had arrived while his father still flourished, expressed amazement that the Romans should hesitate to approach the wall. He himself was a born fighter, naturally venturesome, and so phenomenally strong that his audacity rarely failed to achieve its end. Titus smiled and said that they were partners in the struggle; so without more ado Antiochus led his Macedonians in a sudden onslaught on the wall. He himself, thanks to his strength and skill, was untouched by the Jewish missiles as he shot his arrows at them. But his youngsters were severely battered, except a very few; for to fulfil their promise they fought tooth and nail, and when they at last retired many had become casualties. No doubt they said to themselves that even real Macedonians could only conquer if they had Alexander's luck!

The Romans had begun work on the 12th of Artemisios, but they only completed the platforms on the 29th, after seventeen days of continuous toil; for all

The Horrors of the Siege

four were of vast size. One, facing Antonia, was raised by the Fifth Legion opposite the middle of the Quince Pool; another, built by the Twelfth, was thirty feet away. A long way from these, to the north of the City, was the work of the Tenth, near the Almond Pool; forty-five feet from this the Fifteenth built theirs by the High Priest's Monument. But from within the City John tunnelled through the ground near Antonia, supporting the galleries with wooden props, and by the time the engines were brought up he had reached the platforms and left the works without solid support. Next he carried in faggots daubed with pitch and bitumen and set them alight, so that as soon as the props were burnt away the entire tunnel collapsed, and with a thunderous crash the platforms fell into the cavity. At once there arose a dense cloud of smoke and dust as the flames were choked by the debris; then when the mass of timber was burnt away a brilliant flame broke through. This sudden blow filled the Romans with consternation, and the ingenuity of the Jews plunged them into despondency; as they had felt sure that victory was imminent, the shock froze their hope of success even in the future. To fight the flames seemed useless, for even if they did put them out their platforms were already swallowed up.

Two days later Simon's forces assaulted the other two platforms; for the Romans had brought up their battering-rams on this side and were already rocking the wall. A certain Tephthaeus, who came from Garis in Galilee, and Magassarus, one of the royal troops and an attendant of Mariamme, accompanied by a man from Adiabene, the son of one Nabataeus, nicknamed Ceagiras, 'the Cripple', because of a disability, picked up firebrands and rushed at the engines. In the whole course of the war the City produced no one more heroic than these three, or more terrifying. They dashed out as if towards friends, not massed enemies; they neither hesitated nor shrank back, but charged through the centre of the foe and set the artillery on fire. Pelted with missiles and thrust at with swords on every side, they refused to withdraw from their perilous situation till the engines were ablaze. When the flames were already shooting up, the Romans came running from the camps to the rescue. But the Jews advanced from the wall to stop them, grappling with those who attempted to quench the flames and utterly disregarding their personal danger. The Romans tugged at the battering-rams while the wicker covers blazed; the Jews, surrounded with the flames, pulled the other way, and seizing the red-hot iron would not leave go of the rams. From these the fire spread to the platforms, outstripping the defenders. Meantime, the Romans were enveloped in flames, and despairing of saving their handiwork began to withdraw to their camps. The Jews pressed them hard, their numbers constantly swelled by reinforcements from the City, and emboldened by their success attacked with the utmost violence till they actually reached the Roman fortifications and engaged the defenders.

There is an armed picket, periodically relieved, which occupies a position in front of every Roman camp and is subject to the very drastic regulation that a man who retires, no matter what the circumstances, must be executed. These men, preferring death with honour to

The Horrors of the Siege

death as a penalty, stood their ground, and their desperate plight shamed many of the runaways into making a stand. Spear-throwers were set up on the wall to drive off the mass of men that poured out of the City without the slightest thought for their own safety. These grappled with all who stood in their path, falling recklessly upon the Roman spears and flinging their very bodies against the foe. It was less by actions than by supreme confidence that they gained the advantage, and it was Jewish audacity rather than their own casualties that made the Romans give ground.

At this crisis Titus arrived from Antonia, to which he had withdrawn to choose a site for more platforms. He expressed the utmost contempt for the soldiers, who after capturing the enemy's walls were in danger of losing their own, and were enduring a siege themselves through letting the Jews out of prison to attack them! Then he put himself at the head of a body of picked men and tried to turn the flank of the enemy, who, although assailed from the front, wheeled round to meet this new threat and resisted stubbornly. In the confusion that followed, blinded by the dust and deafened by the uproar, neither side could distinguish friend from foe. The Jews stood firm, not so much through prowess now as through despair of victory; the Romans were braced by respect for the honour of their arms, especially as Caesar was in the forefront of danger. The struggle would probably have ended, such was the fury of the Romans, with the capture of the whole mass of Jews, had they not forestalled the crisis of the battle by retreating to the City. With their platforms destroyed the Romans were

The Fall of Jerusalem

downhearted, having lost the fruits of their prolonged labours in a single hour; many indeed felt that with conventional weapons they would never take the City.

Titus held a council of war. The more sanguine spirits were for bringing the whole army into action in a full-scale assault. Hitherto only a fraction of their forces had been engaged with the enemy; if they advanced en masse the Jews would yield to the first onslaught, overwhelmed by the rain of missiles. The more cautious urged either that they should reconstruct the platforms, or that, abandoning them, they should merely blockade the City and prevent the inhabitants from making sallies or bringing in food, leaving them to starve and refraining from combat. For there was no battling with despair, when men desired only to die by the sword and so escape a more horrible fate. Titus himself thought it unwise to let so large a force remain idle, while there was no point in fighting those who were certain to destroy each other. To throw up platforms was a hopeless task with timber so scarce, to prevent sallies still more hopeless. For to form a ring of men round so big a City and over such difficult terrain was impracticable, and highly dangerous in view of sudden attacks. The known paths might be blocked, but the Jews would contrive secret ways out, driven by necessity and knowing the ground. Again, if provisions were smuggled in, the siege would be prolonged still further, and he was afraid that the lustre of his triumph would be dimmed by its slowness in coming. Given time, anything could be accomplished, but reputations were won by speed. If he was to combine speed with safety he must build a wall round the entire

The Horrors of the Siege

City. That was the only way to block every exit and force the Jews to abandon their last hope of survival and surrender the City. If they did not, hunger would make them easy victims. For he would not wait for things to happen, but would resume construction of the platforms when resistance had been weakened. If anyone thought the task too great to carry out, he must remember that little tasks were beneath the dignity of Rome, and that without hard work nothing great could be achieved, unless by a miracle.

Having thus convinced the generals, Titus ordered them to divide up the work between their units. An inspired enthusiasm seized the soldiers, and when the circuit had been marked out there was competition not only between legions but even between cohorts. The private was eager to please his decurion, the decurion his centurion, the centurion his tribune; the tribunes were ambitious for the praise of the generals; and of the rivalry between the generals Caesar himself was judge. He personally went round several times every day to inspect the work. Starting at the Assyrians' Camp, where his own quarters were, he took the wall to the New City below, and from there across the Kidron to the Mount of Olives. Then he bent the line towards the south enclosing the Mount (as far as the rock called the Dovecot) and the next eminence, which overhangs the valley near Siloam. From there he went in a westerly direction down into Fountain Valley, then up by the tomb of Ananus the high priest, embracing the hill where Pompey's camp had been. Then turning north he passed the village called The House of Peas, and rounding

Herod's Tomb went east till he finished up at his own camp, the starting-place. The wall measured 4½ miles, and outside were built on thirteen forts with a combined circumference of over a mile. Yet the whole task was completed in three days, though it might well have taken months – the speed passed belief. Having surrounded the City with this wall and garrisoned the forts, Titus himself took the first night watch and went the rounds; the second he entrusted to Alexander; the third was assigned to the legion commanders. The guards drew lots for periods of sleep, and all night long they patrolled the intervals between the forts.

The Jews, unable to leave the City, were deprived of all hope of survival. The famine became more intense and devoured whole houses and families. The roofs were covered with women and babies too weak to stand, the streets full of old men already dead. Young men and boys, swollen with hunger, haunted the squares like ghosts and fell wherever faintness overcame them. To bury their kinsfolk was beyond the strength of the sick, and those who were fit shirked the task because of the number of the dead and uncertainty about their own fate; for many while burying others fell dead themselves, and many set out for their graves before their hour struck. In their misery no weeping or lamentation was heard; hunger stifled emotion; with dry eyes and grinning mouths those who were slow to die watched those whose end came sooner. Deep silence enfolded the City, and a darkness burdened with death. Worse still were the bandits, who broke into the houses of the dead like tomb-robbers, stripped the bodies, snatching off their wrappings, and then came out laughing. They tried the points of their swords on the corpses, and even transfixed some of those who lay helpless but still alive, to test the steel. But if any begged for a swordthrust to end their sufferings, they contemptuously left them to die of hunger. Everyone as he breathed his last fixed his eyes on the Sanctuary, turning his back on the partisans he was leaving alive. The latter at first ordered the dead to be buried at public expense as they could not bear the stench; later, when this proved impossible, they threw them from the walls into the valleys. When in the course of his rounds Titus saw these choked with dead, and a putrid stream trickling from under the decomposing bodies, he groaned, and uplifting his hands called God to witness that this was not his doing.

While such were the conditions in the City, the Romans were exuberant, for none of the partisans sallied out now that they too were despondent and hungry. There was an abundance of corn and other necessities from Syria and the neighbouring provinces, and the soldiers delighted to stand near the wall and display their ample supplies of food, by their own abundance inflaming the hunger of the enemy. But when suffering made the partisans no more ready to submit, Titus took pity on the remnant of the people, and in his anxiety to rescue the survivors again began constructing platforms, though it was difficult to get timber. Round the City it had all been cut down for the previous works, and the soldiers had to collect new supplies from more than ten miles away. Concentrating on Antonia, they raised platforms in four sections, much bigger than the earlier ones. Caesar made the round of the legions, speeding the work and showing the bandits they were in his hands. But they alone seemed to have lost all sense of remorse, and making a division between soul and body acted as if neither belonged to them. For their souls were as insensitive to suffering as their bodies were to pain – they tore the carcase of the nation with their fangs, and filled the prisons with the defenceless.

Simon actually put Matthias, who had made him master of the City, to death by torture. He was a member of a high-priestly family, the son of Boethus, and he enjoyed the absolute trust and respect of the people. When the masses were being roughly handled by the Zealots whom John had already joined, he persuaded the people to accept Simon's aid, having made no pact with him but expecting no mischief from him. When however Simon arrived and got the City into his power, he treated Matthias as an enemy like the rest, and the furtherer of his cause as a mere simpleton. Matthias was brought before him and accused of favouring the Romans, and without being allowed to defend himself, was condemned to die with three of his sons. The fourth had already made his escape to Titus. When Matthias begged to be killed before his children, pleading for this as a favour because he had opened the gates to Simon, the monster ordered him to be killed last. So his sons were murdered before his eyes and then his dead body was thrown on to theirs, in full view of the Romans. Such were the instructions that Simon had given to Ananus, son of Bagadates, the most brutal of his henchmen; and he mockingly enquired whether Matthias

The Horrors of the Siege

hoped for assistance from his new friends. Burial of the bodies was forbidden. After their deaths an eminent priest named Ananias, son of Masbalus, and the clerk of the Sanhedrin, Aristaeus, whose home was Emmaus, together with fifteen distinguished citizens, were put to death. Josephus' father was kept under lock and key, and an edict forbade anyone in the City to associate with him through fear of betrayal. Any who condoled with him were executed without trial.

Seeing all this Judas, son of Judas, a subordinate whom Simon had entrusted with command of a tower, partly through disgust at these brutal murders but chiefly with an eye to his own safety, collected the ten most reliable of his men. 'How long,' he asked, 'shall we endure these horrors? What hope of survival have we if we remain loyal to a scoundrel? We are starving already and the Romans have almost got in. Simon is betraying his best friends and is likely soon to jump on us; but the word of the Romans can be trusted. So come on! Let us surrender the wall and save ourselves and the City! Simon had lost hope already! It won't hurt him if he gets his deserts a bit sooner.' This argument convinced the ten, and at dawn he sent off the rest in different directions to avoid discovery. Three hours later he shouted from his tower to the Romans, but some of them were scornful, others mistrustful, the majority uninterested: in any case the City would soon fall into their lap. Titus advanced with his heavy infantry towards the wall. But Simon stole a march on him, occupied the tower first, arrested the men, executed them before the eyes of the Romans, and threw their mutilated bodies over the wall.

At this time, as he went round making yet another appeal, Josephus was struck on the head by a stone and fell to the ground unconscious. Seeing him fall the Jews ran out, and would have dragged him into the City had not Caesar promptly sent men to protect him. While they fought Josephus was picked up, knowing little of what was going on. The partisans thought they had disposed of the man they hated most, and whooped for joy. When the report spread through the City, the survivors of the populace were overcome with despair, believing that they had really lost the man with whose help they hoped to desert. When Josephus' mother was told in prison that her son was dead, she said to the guards that she had foreseen this ever since Jotapata; while he was alive she might as well have had no son. Privately she lamented to her maids that this was the only result of bringing children into the world – she would not even bury the son whom she had expected to bury her. But the false report neither grieved her nor cheered the bandits for long. Josephus soon recovered from the blow, and went forward to shout that it would not be long before they paid the penalty for wounding him, and to implore the people to trust him. His reappearance brought new hope to the common folk, to the partisans' consternation.

Some of the deserters, seeing no other way, promptly jumped from the wall. Others advanced as if to battle armed with stones, then fled to the Romans. Their fate was worse than if they had stayed in the City, and the hunger they had left behind was, as they discovered, less lethal than the plenty the Romans provided. They arrived

The Horrors of the Siege

blown up by starvation as if by dropsy, then stuffed their empty bellies non-stop till they burst – except for those who were wise enough to restrain their appetites and take the unaccustomed food a little at a time. Those who escaped this danger fell victims to another disaster. In the Syrian camp one deserter was caught picking gold coins out of his excreta. As I mentioned, they swallowed coins before leaving, because they were all searched by the partisans, and there was a great deal of gold in the City. In fact it fetched less than half the old price. But when the trick was discovered through one man, the rumour ran round the camps that the deserters were arriving stuffed with gold. The Arab unit and the Syrians cut open the refugees and ransacked their bellies. To me this seems the most terrible calamity that happened to the Jews: in a single night nearly two thousand were ripped up.

When Titus learnt of this atrocity he was on the point of surrounding the perpetrators with his cavalry and shooting them down. But far too many were involved; in fact those to be punished far outnumbered their victims. Instead he summoned both the auxiliary and the legionary commanders, some of whose men were accused of participating, and spoke angrily to both groups. Was it possible that some of his own soldiers did such things on the off chance of gain, and had no respect for their own weapons that were made of silver and gold? The Arabs and Syrians, serving in a war that was not the concern of their own nation, began by indulging their passions in an undisciplined fashion, and ended by letting Romans take the blame for their bloodthirsty butchery and their hatred for the Jews; for some of his own soldiers shared their evil reputation. The foreigners therefore he threatened to punish with death if any man was caught after this committing such a crime. The legionary commanders he instructed to ferret out suspected offenders and bring them before him.

But avarice, it seems, scorns every penalty and an extraordinary love of gain is innate in man, nor is any emotion as strong as covetousness. At other times these passions are kept within bounds and over-awed by fear. But it was God who condemned the whole nation and turned every means of escape to their destruction. So what Caesar forebade with threats was still done to the deserters in secret, and the refugees, before the rest noticed them, were met and murdered by the foreign soldiers, who looked round in case any Roman saw them, then ripped them up and pulled the filthy money out of their bowels. In few however was any found, the majority being victims of an empty hope. Fear of this fate caused many of the deserters to return.

When there was nothing left that John could extort from the people, he turned to sacrilege and melted down many of the offerings in the Sanctuary and many of the vessels required for services, basins, dishes, and tables, not even keeping his hands off the flagons presented by Augustus and his consort. For the Roman emperors honoured and adorned the Temple at all times. But now this Jew stole even the gifts of foreigners, telling his companions that they need not hesitate to use God's property for God's benefit, and that those who fought for the Sanctuary were entitled to live on it. Accordingly

The Horrors of the Siege

he emptied out the sacred corn and oil which the priests kept in the inner court of the Temple to pour on burnt offerings, and shared them out to the crowd, who without a qualm swallowed a pailful or smeared it on themselves. I cannot refrain from saying what my feelings dictate. I think that if the Romans had delayed their attack on these sacrilegious ruffians, either the ground would have opened and swallowed up the City, or a flood would have overwhelmed it, or lightning would have destroyed it like Sodom. For it produced a generation far more godless than those who perished thus, a generation whose mad folly involved the nation in ruin.

But why should I describe these calamities one by one? While they were happening Mannaeus, son of Lazarus, fled to Titus and told him that through a single gate which had been entrusted to him 115,880 corpses had been carried out between the 14th of Xanthicos, when the Romans pitched their camp near the city, and the 1st of Panemos. All these were the bodies of paupers. Though he was not himself in charge, he had to pay the expenses out of public funds, and so was obliged to keep count. The rest were buried by their own kin, who merely brought them out and threw them clear of the City. After Mannaeus many distinguished citizens deserted, and these reported that in all 600,000 pauper bodies had been thrown out at the gates: of the others the number was unknown. When it was no longer possible to carry out the penniless, they said, the corpses had been heaped up in the biggest houses and the doors locked. The price of corn was fantastically high, and now that the City was walled round and they could not even gather herbs, some were in such dire straits that they raked the sewers and old dunghills and swallowed the refuse they found there, so that what once they could not bear to look at now became their food.

When the Romans heard of all this misery they felt pity: the partisans, who saw it with their own eyes, showed no regrets but allowed these things to come upon them too; for they were blinded by the doom that was closing in on the City and on themselves.

Antonia Captured and Destroyed

As the days wore on the plight of Jerusalem grew steadily worse, the partisans being goaded to greater fury by successive calamities, while the famine that devoured the people now preyed on themselves. The innumerable corpses piled up all over the City not merely were a revolting sight and emitted a pestilential stench: they obstructed the fighting-men as they made their sorties; for like men marching across a battlefield littered with thousands of dead they were forced to trample on the bodies. But as they trod them underfoot they gave no shudder, felt no pity, and saw no ill omen to themselves in this insult to the departed. Their hands drenched with their country's blood, they rushed out to battle with foreigners, reproaching the Almighty, it seems to me, for His slowness in punishing them; for it was not hope of victory but despair of deliverance now that emboldened them for the fight. The Romans, though it was a terrible struggle to collect the timber, raised their platforms in twenty-one days, having, as described before, stripped the whole area in a circle round the town to a distance of ten miles. The countryside like the City was a pitiful sight; for where once there had been a lovely vista of woods and parks there was now nothing but desert and the stumps of trees. No one – not even a foreigner – who had seen the old Judaea and the glorious suburbs of the City, and now set eyes on her present desolation, could have helped sighing and groaning at so terrible a change; for every trace of beauty had been blotted out by the war, and nobody who had known it in the past and came upon it suddenly would have recognized the place: he would have gone on looking for the City when he was already in it.

To Romans and Jews alike the completion of the platforms brought a new terror. The Jews felt sure that unless they burnt these too the City would fall, the Romans that it would never be taken if they went the way of the others. For no more timber was available, and the soldiers' physical strength had been sapped by toil and their morale by constant reverses. Indeed, the disastrous conditions in the City proved more discouraging to the Romans than to the inhabitants: they found the fighting-men not in the least subdued by their severe reverses, while their own hopes were continually frustrated, their platforms rendered useless by stratagems, their engines by the strength of the wall, and their skill in close combat by the daring of their adversaries. Worst blow of all, they discovered that the Jews had an inner courage that rose superior to faction, famine, war, and disasters beyond number. They began to think the onslaughts of these men irresistible, and their equanimity amidst disasters unshakable – what would they not endure if fortune favoured them, seeing that calamity only whetted their appetite for battle? Small wonder, then, that the Romans made the guard-posts of the platforms stronger still.

John's forces in Antonia were building up their

Antonia Captured and Destroyed

strength for eventualities, in case the wall was thrown down. At the same time they forestalled the onslaught of the rams by an assault on the Roman earthworks. The attempt was a failure: they advanced torch in hand, but before nearing the platforms lost hope completely and turned back. In the first place there seemed to be no agreed plan – they dashed out a few at a time, at intervals, with hesitation and fear – in short, unlike Jews; there was little sign of the national characteristics, boldness, dash, the massed charge and the refusal to acknowledge defeat. But while the customary vigour was lacking in their advance, they found the Romans formed up in unusual strength; with their mail-clad bodies they surrounded the platforms with so complete a bulwark as to leave no chink anywhere for the passage of a firebrand, and every man braced himself to die rather than budge from his post. For apart from the destruction of all their hopes if these works too went up in flames, the soldiers could not bear the thought that trickery should triumph every time over prowess, desperation over skill at arms, numbers over experience, and Jews over Romans. Furthermore the artillery co-operated by dropping missiles on the leading Jewish files: the fallen held up those immediately behind, and the risk of going to the fore quenched their ardour. Of those who pushed beyond the beaten zone, some before coming to close quarters took fright at the disciplined and serried ranks of the enemy, others took to flight only when pricked by their lances. At last flinging the word 'coward' at each other, they withdrew with nothing to show. It was on the 1st of Panemos that the attempt was made.

The Fall of Jerusalem

After the Jewish withdrawal the Romans brought up the battering-rams, though they were being pelted with lumps of rock from Antonia, with firebrands, arrows, and every weapon with which necessity furnished the Jews; for though they felt sure of their wall and despised the engines, they nevertheless tried to prevent them from being brought up. The Romans, assuming that the anxiety of the Jews to avert an assault on Antonia was due to the weakness of the wall, and hoping that the foundations were unsound, made strenuous counter-efforts. The wall stood up to the blows, but the Romans under a deluge of missiles paid no heed to any danger from above and kept the battering-rams constantly at work. As, however, they were awkwardly placed and crushed by the lumps of rock, other men working under a roof of shields strove with hands and crowbars to undermine the foundations, and by strenuous efforts levered out four stones. Darkness ended the activities of both sides, but in the night, at the point where John had undermined the wall by the measures which he had devised against the earlier platforms, the tunnel fell in and the wall, already shaken by the rams, suddenly collapsed.

This occurrence had an astonishing effect on both sides. The Jews, who might have been expected to lose heart because the collapse was unlooked for and they were unprepared for it, took it quite calmly as Antonia remained; but the Romans' unlooked for delight at the downfall was quickly extinguished by the sight of another wall which John's men had built just behind. Certainly this one appeared easier to assail than the other: to climb

Antonia Captured and Destroyed

up over the ruins seemed a simple matter, and it was assumed that the wall was much weaker than that of Antonia, and that as it had been erected in an emergency it would quickly disintegrate. However, no one dared to climb up: for those who led the way it meant certain death.

Believing that zest for battle is roused most effectively by words of encouragement, and that incentives and promises often make men oblivious of danger, sometimes contemptuous of death itself, Titus got together the élite of his army and put them to the test.

'My fellow-soldiers,' he began, 'to urge men on to actions involving no risk is a deliberate insult to them and an unmistakable proof of the speaker's cowardice. Incentives, surely, are needed only for dangerous enterprises: the other sort men will undertake without any inducement. So I tell you here and now that the ascent to this wall is a formidable task: the point I would emphasize is that the first duty of those who pride themselves on their courage is to battle with difficulties, that it is a splendid thing to die with honour, and that the heroism of those who lead the way will be amply rewarded. In the first place, what might well be a deterrent to some should be an incentive to you – the endurance of these Jews and their fortitude in distress. It would be scandalous for men who are Romans and my soldiers, in peacetime trained for war, in war accustomed to triumph, to be outshone by Jews in strength or determination, and that on the brink of victory and with God to assist us! For our setbacks are the result of Jewish desperation; their difficulties are increased both by your prowess and by God's assistance. Faction, hunger, siege, walls that fall when no engine is at work – what else can be the cause but God's anger with them and co-operation with ourselves? So to be outdone by our inferiors and to betray God our Ally as well would be unworthy of us. It would be utterly disgraceful that Jews, whose reputation suffers little from defeat as they have learnt to endure slavery, should despise death in order to escape from it and repeatedly sally out against our full strength, not in the hope of victory but merely to prove their courage, while you, the lords of almost every land and sea, who could not hold up your heads if victory escaped you, never once hazarded a direct encounter with the enemy, but waited for starvation or bad luck to bring them to their knees, while you sat idle with such weapons in your hands, and that when at a trifling hazard you could win a resounding victory! Once we are on top of Antonia, the City is at our mercy; for even if there is some further fighting against the men inside – I do not anticipate any – we shall be sitting on top, squeezing the breath out of them; and that means victory, speedy and complete.

'I have no intention at this moment of singing the praises of death in battle and the immortality given to those who are killed when fighting-mad; as for those who are not made that way, curse them, I hope they will die in a bed of disease, condemned body and soul to the grave. For every good soldier knows that souls set free from the flesh on the battlefield by the sword are given a welcome by the purest element, ether, and set among the stars, and that as friendly spirits and genial

Antonia Captured and Destroyed

heroes they appear to their own descendants; while souls that waste away in sick bodies, even if completely free from spots and stains, vanish into darkness underground and sink deep into oblivion, life, body, and memory too annihilated at one stroke. But if it is fated that all men must die and the sword is a kindlier minister of death than any sickness, how contemptible it would be not to give to the service of our country what we must yield up to fate!

'I have spoken so far as if those who make the attempt cannot possibly come through alive; but it *is* possible for those who play the man to come safely through the very greatest dangers. First, the ruined wall will be easy to climb; then all the new structure will be easy to throw down. More and more of you must call up your courage for the task and give each other encouragement and support; your determination will soon take the heart out of the Jews. It is quite possible that you will win a bloodless victory once you take the first step. As you climb they will presumably try to stop you; but if you once force your way through undetected, there will be no further resistance, even if only a few of you get there. As for the man who takes the lead, I should be ashamed if when honours are awarded I did not make him an object of envy. Finally the survivor shall be promoted over his present equals, and the fallen shall receive the coveted meed of valour.'

Listening to this speech the bulk of the army were appalled by the greatness of the danger; but in one of the cohorts there was a man called Sabinus, a Syrian by race, who in prowess and courage proved himself

The Fall of Jerusalem

outstanding. And yet anyone who had seen him before would have concluded from his physical appearance that he was not even an average soldier. His skin was black, his flesh lean and shrunken; but in his frail body, far too slender for its own prowess, dwelt a heroic soul. Springing to his feet he cried: 'I gladly offer you my services, Caesar. I am the first to scale the wall. I trust my strength and determination will have the benefit of your usual luck; but if I am thwarted in my efforts, rest assured I am quite prepared for failure and for your sake have chosen death with my eyes open.'

So saying, with his left hand he held his shield in front of and over his head, and drawing his sword with his right stepped out towards the wall, just about midday. He was followed by eleven of the others, the only ones to emulate his courage; but he went on far ahead of them all, driven by some supernatural impulse. The guards on the battlements flung spears at them, discharged volleys of arrows from all directions and rolled down great lumps of rock, which swept away some of the eleven; but Sabinus, charging into the missiles and buried under the arrows, did not falter for a moment till he had got to the top and routed the enemy. For the Jews, astounded by his dynamic energy and remorseless determination, and thinking too that others had climbed up, turned tail. And here one might well complain of Fortune, so jealous of heroic deeds and ever ready to prevent brilliant successes. For this brave man, just as he achieved his purpose, tripped up, and stumbling over a big stone fell flat on top of it with a great crash. The Jews swung round, and seeing him alone and on the

Antonia Captured and Destroyed

ground pelted him from all directions. He got up on one knee, and covering himself with his shield for a time fought back, wounding many who came near him; but soon, riddled with wounds, he lost the use of his right hand and at length, before he breathed his last, he was buried under the arrows. So brave a man deserved a better fate, yet his fall was a fitting end to such an enterprise. Of the others, three who had already reached the top were battered to death with stones, the other eight were dragged down wounded and carried back to camp. This incident took place on the 3rd of Panemos.

Two days later twenty of the men guarding the advanced posts on the platforms got together, and calling on the standard-bearer of the Fifth Legion, two soldiers from the cavalry squadrons and one trumpeter, at 2 a.m. moved forward in silence through the ruins of Antonia. Disposing of the first sentries in their sleep, they got possession of the wall and ordered the trumpeter to sound. The other guards instantly leapt to their feet and ran away without staying to see how many had climbed up; for the trumpet-call and the resulting panic deluded them into thinking that the enemy had climbed up en masse. When Caesar heard the signal he armed his forces with all speed, and with his generals and picked troops led the way to the top. The Jews had taken refuge in the Temple, and the Romans poured in through the tunnel which John had dug to the Roman platforms. The partisans of both groups, John's and Simon's, drawn up separately, blocked their way, displaying strength and determination to the very limit; they realized that a Roman entry into the Sanctuary would be the beginning

The Fall of Jerusalem

of the end, while the Romans saw in it the dawn of victory. Round the entrances they grappled in a life and death struggle, the Romans driving on relentlessly to get possession of the Temple, the Jews pushing them back towards Antonia. Arrows and spears were of no use to either side; they drew their swords and closed; in the milling mass it was impossible to distinguish one side from the other, as the men were locked together inextricably in the confined space, and amidst the uproar their shouts conveyed no meaning to the ear. The carnage on both sides was terrible, and the mail-clad bodies of the fallen were trampled and crushed by the combatants. Whichever way the tide of battle swung, the cheers of the victors and the groans of the routed were always to be heard. There was room for neither flight nor pursuit: in the confused struggle the turns of the scale, the movements this way and that, were infinitesimal. Those in front must either kill or be killed – there could be no retreat; for on either side those behind pressed their own men forward and left no space between the opposing lines. But the time came when Jewish fury got the better of Roman skill and the line began to give from end to end. After all, they had fought without a break from 2 a.m. till 1 p.m., the Jews in full strength and with the danger of utter defeat as a spur to their valour, the Romans with only a tiny part of their army, since the legions which the men actually fighting counted on had not yet followed them up the slope. So it was sufficient for the present to be in possession of Antonia.

Standing by Titus' side in Antonia was a centurion from Bithynia called Julianus, a man of note and far

Antonia Captured and Destroyed

more remarkable for skill in arms, physical strength, and fearless spirit than anyone I met with from beginning to end of the war. When he saw the Romans already giving way and putting up a poor defence, he sprang forward and drove back the already victorious Jews, unaided, as far as the corner of the inner court of the Temple. The whole mass fled, convinced that such strength and audacity could not be those of a mere man. This way and that he charged through their midst as they scattered, killing all he could reach: never had Caesar beheld so amazing a sight, or the other side one so terrifying. But he too was pursued by Fate, from whom there is no escape for mortal man. He was wearing the ordinary military boots studded with masses of sharp nails, and as he ran across the stone pavement he slipped and fell flat on his back, his armour clanging so loudly that the runaways turned to look. A shout went up from the Romans in Antonia, alarmed for their champion's safety, while the Jews crowded round him and aimed blows from all directions with their lances and broadswords. Many heavy blows he stopped with his shield; time after time he tried to stand up but was knocked down by the mass of assailants. Even then as he lay he stabbed many with his sword; for he could not be finished off easily, as he was protected in every vital part by helmet and breastplate and kept his head down. But at last, when all his limbs were slashed and no one dared come to his aid, he ceased to struggle.

Caesar was greatly distressed at the death of so gallant a soldier, killed before so many eyes. He himself was prevented by his situation from going to the rescue,

The Fall of Jerusalem

though anxious to do so. Those who might have gone were too terrified. So Julianus, after a long fight for life in which he allowed few of his assailants to go unscathed, at long last received the *coup de grâce*, leaving behind him, not only with Caesar but even with his foes, a glorious reputation. The Jews snatched the body and again drove the Romans back, shutting them up in Antonia. Those on their side who distinguished themselves in this battle were Alexas and Gyphthaeus among John's followers, among Simon's Malachias, Judas, son of Merto, and Jacob, son of Sosas, commanding the Idumaeans, and of the Zealots two brothers, sons of Jairus, by name Simon and Judas.

Titus ordered the soldiers with him to lay Antonia flat and make the ascent easy for the whole army. Then he put up Josephus to speak; for he was informed that on that day, the 17th of Panemos, through lack of lambs the so-called Continual Sacrifice had been discontinued, and that the people were consequently in the depths of despair. Josephus was to make John the same offer as before: if he was possessed by some morbid craving for a fight, he was free to come out with as many men as he liked and join battle without at the same time bringing destruction on the City and Sanctuary; but he must stop polluting the Holy Place and offending against God. Moreover he was permitted to choose any Jews he liked to offer the discontinued sacrifices.

Josephus took his stand where he could be heard not only by John but by the masses and delivered Caesar's message in Aramaic, appealing to them eloquently to spare their birthplace, to beat out the flames already

Antonia Captured and Destroyed

enveloping the Sanctuary and to restore to God the due oblations. Listening to him the people remained silent and dejected; but the chief gangster poured abuse and curses on the head of Josephus, finally adding that he would never be afraid of capture, as the City was God's. Josephus loudly retorted:

'Of course, you have kept it perfectly pure for God, and the Holy Place remains unpolluted! You have never dishonoured your hoped-for Ally! He still receives the customary sacrifices! If anyone robbed you of your daily food, you godless creature, you would regard him as your enemy; and do you think you can count on God, whom you have denied His everlasting worship, to be your Ally in the war? And do you blame your own sins on the Romans, who have throughout respected our Law and are now pressing you to restore to God the sacrifices which you have interrupted? Who would not groan with anguish at the astounding change that has come over the City, when foreigners and enemies atone for your ungodliness and you, a Jew, cradled in the Law, do more hurt than they? But consider, John! To turn your back on evil ways is no disgrace, even at the last moment. If you wish to save your birthplace, you have a splendid example before you in Jehoiachin, king of the Jews. When the king of Babylon made war on him through his own fault, he left the city of his own accord before its capture, and with his family submitted to voluntary imprisonment rather than surrender these holy places to the enemy and see the House of God go up in flames. For that he is celebrated by all Jews in the sacred record, and memory, flowing through the

The Fall of Jerusalem

ages eternally new, passes him on to future generations immortal. A splendid example, John, even if it were dangerous! But I can guarantee your pardon from the Romans. Remember, this is the advice of a fellow-countryman and the promise of a Jew; it is sensible to consider who is counselling you and where he comes from. I trust that never while I live shall I become such an abject slave as to deny my birth or forget my heritage!

'Once more you rage against me with loud-mouthed abuse. I deserve even worse for flying in the face of fate to advise you, and fighting to save men damned by God. Who doesn't know the writings of the old prophets and the oracle pronounced against this unhappy city and now about to be fulfilled? They foretold the day of her fall – the day when some man began the slaughter of his fellow countrymen. And aren't the City and Temple full of your dead bodies? It is God then, God Himself who is bringing with the Romans fire to purge the Temple and is blotting out the City, brimful of corruption, as if it had never been.'

As Josephus spoke thus, with groanings and tears, sobs choked his voice. Even the Romans were moved by his distress and applauded his determination; but John's party were the more incensed with the Romans, and mad to get Josephus into their clutches. However, many citizens of good family were shaken by his speech. Some of them were too frightened of the partisan guards to move, though they had given up themselves and the City for lost; but a few watched their opportunity to escape and sought asylum with the Romans. These included the chief priests Joseph and Jeshua and several sons of chief priests, three sons of Ishmael, who was beheaded in Cyrene, four of Matthias and one of another Matthias; this man had run away after the death of his father, who had been murdered by Simon, son of Gioras, with three sons, as explained above. Many other citizens of good family went over with the chief priests. Caesar received them with all possible kindness, and knowing that foreign customs would make life distasteful for them he sent them to Gophna, where he advised them to remain for the time being: he would restore every man's possessions as soon as he had got the war off his hands. So they retired to the little town allotted to them in perfect safety and supremely content.

When they did not reappear, the partisans again spread the tale that the Romans had butchered the deserters, obviously in the hope that the rest would be too frightened to run away. As before, the trick worked for a time; terror effectively put a stop to desertions. But when the men were brought back from Gophna by Titus and ordered to go round the wall with Josephus under the eyes of the people, there was a wholesale flight to the Romans. All the fugitives joined together, and standing in front of the Roman lines wept and wailed as they besought the partisans, if they could bring themselves to do it, to fling their gates wide open to the Romans; if not, at least to withdraw from the Temple and save their Sanctuary: the Romans would never bring themselves, unless absolutely driven to it, to burn down the sacred buildings. This appeal provoked a violent reaction; a volley of abuse was hurled at the deserters, and above the sacred gates spear-throwers, catapults, and stone-

The Fall of Jerusalem

throwers were set in line, so that the Temple courts, littered with bodies, were like a vast graveyard, the Sanctuary itself like a fortress. Into the sacred, untrodden precincts they poured armed to the teeth, their hands still dripping with the blood of their own countrymen. So monstrous was their conduct that the indignation the Jews might well have felt, if the Romans had committed such outrages against them, was felt by the Romans now against the Jews who profaned their own holy ground. In fact, among the soldiers there was not a man who was not filled with reverent awe when his eyes rested on the Sanctuary, or who did not pray that the terrorists would see the light before all was lost. Greatly distressed, Titus again reproached John and his supporters.

'You disgusting people! Didn't you put up that balustrade to guard your Holy House? Didn't you at intervals along it place slabs inscribed in Greek characters and our own, forbidding anyone to go beyond the parapet? And didn't we give you leave to execute anyone who did go beyond it, even if he was a Roman? Why then, you guilty men, are you now trampling dead bodies inside it? Why are you polluting your Sanctuary with the blood of foreigner and native? I call the gods of my fathers and any god that ever watched over this place – I do not believe there is one now – I call my own army, the Jews in my camp, and you yourselves to witness that *I* am not compelling you to desecrate your Temple. If you change the battle-ground, no Roman shall go near your holy places or insult them: I will protect the Sanctuary for you, whether you wish it or not.'

As Josephus made known this promise on Caesar's

Antonia Captured and Destroyed

behalf, the terrorists and their chief, assuming that not good-will but cowardice lay behind his exhortations, received them with scorn. When Titus saw that these men had no mercy on themselves and no concern for the Sanctuary, he resumed hostilities, though much against his will. It was not possible to bring up his whole army against them as there was not room enough; so he picked out from every century the thirty best soldiers and put a tribune in charge of every thousand, the entire force being under the command of Cerealis, with orders to attack the guardposts an hour before sunrise. He was himself in arms and ready to go down with them, but his friends held him back because the danger was so great, and because the officers insisted that he would do more good by sitting quietly in Antonia in general control of the operations of his men than by going down into the forefront of the battle; if Caesar was watching every man would fight to the death. Yielding to their arguments Caesar explained to the men that he was staying behind for one purpose only – to be judge of their exploits, so that no brave man should go unrewarded, no coward unpunished, through not being seen, and to be an eyewitness of every deed, able as he was both to punish and to reward. So he sent them to their task at the time mentioned above, and going himself to an excellent forward observation-post he remained in Antonia, anxiously awaiting the outcome.

However, the task-force did not find the guards asleep, as they hoped; they leapt to their feet with loud yells and a hand-to-hand struggle instantly began. When the shout of the sentries was heard within, the rest of the guard poured out in a body. Under the onslaught of the leading ranks the Romans stood firm; those who followed collided with their own troops and many treated friends as foes. They could not distinguish voices because of the confused hubbub, nor faces because it was night. They were blinded also, some by fury, some by fear; consequently they struck out indiscriminately at all in their path. The Romans locked their shields together and charged in their units, so suffering less from this bewilderment; and every man remembered the password. The Jews were continually scattering, their attacks and retreats were haphazard, and they repeatedly took each other for enemies; in the darkness any man who moved to the rear was invariably received by his friends as an advancing Roman. In fact more were wounded by their comrades than by the enemy, till day broke and it was possible to see what was happening in the battle. The two sides now separated into opposing formations and began to hurl missiles in an orderly engagement. Neither side gave an inch or showed any sign of weariness. The Romans, as Caesar was watching, individually and by companies vied with each other, every man convinced that his promotion would date from that day if he distinguished himself in the fight: the Jews had as judge of their prowess their fear for themselves and for the Temple, and the tyrant who stood over them rousing them to action, some with encouragement, some with threats or the lash. In the main the battle was stationary, the ebb and flow very slight and very rapid: flight and pursuit were alike impossible. All the time the shouts from Antonia changed with the fortunes of their own

Antonia Captured and Destroyed

men: at every advance they were loudly cheered, at every retreat they were urged to stand fast. It was like a battle in an amphitheatre: Titus and his staff could see every detail of the fighting. At last, after battling from before dawn to nearly midday, they broke off the fight, without either side having really budged the other from the spot where the first blow was struck, and without any decision being reached. On the Roman side many had fought magnificently; on the Jewish, of Simon's followers Judas, son of Merto, and Simon, son of Josiah, of the Idumaeans Jacob and Simon, sons of Sosas and Cathla respectively, of John's men Gyphthaeus and Alexas, and of the Zealots Simon, son of Jairus.

Meanwhile the rest of the Roman army had in one week laid Antonia flat and engineered a wide road to the Temple. Advancing near to the first rampart the legions now set to work on four platforms, one opposite the north-west corner of the inner court of the Temple, one near the northern arcade between the two gates, and of the other two one opposite the western colonnade of the outer court, the other farther out opposite the northern. The progress of the work, however, cost them much toil and sweat, as they had to fetch the timber from over eleven miles away. Sometimes they suffered losses through Jewish stratagems, as their crushing superiority made them over-confident just when despair of survival made the Jews more daring than ever. For instance some of the mounted men, every time they went out to collect firewood or fodder, used to let their horses graze free and unbridled while they were foraging; these the Jews would seize and carry off by a sudden sortie in strength.

This happened so often that Caesar, correctly diagnosing the cause of these losses as less the valour of the Jews than the negligence of his own soldiers, decided to take a measure of unusual severity to ensure better care of the horses in future. He commanded one of the men who had lost their mounts to be led off for execution, so terrifying the rest that he made sure their horses would be safe. They never again left them behind to graze, but took them on all their forays as if horse and rider were one. So the war against the Temple continued and the platforms neared completion.

The very day after the advance of the legions many of the partisans, as the supply of loot was running out and hunger was pressing, made a united attack on the Roman posts on the Mount of Olives an hour before sunset, hoping that they would catch them off their guard and already busy with their personal needs, and so force their way through without difficulty. But the Romans saw them coming, and instantly closing in from the neighbouring guard-posts prevented them from climbing over the camp wall or cutting through it by force. There followed a fierce struggle, with many instances of heroic courage on both sides, the Romans showing a combination of strength and tactical skill, the Jews unlimited vigour and uncontrollable fury. Shame was in command of one side, necessity of the other: to let the Jews slip out of the net that enveloped them seemed to the Romans an appalling disgrace: their opponents had one solitary hope of survival – to break through the wall by sheer force. A mounted man from one cohort, by name Pedanius, seeing the Jews at last

Antonia Captured and Destroyed

routed and pushed down into the valley, drove his horse alongside at a furious pace and snatched up one of the enemy as he fled, a young man of sturdy build and in full armour too, seizing him by the ankle – so far did he lean over from the saddle, so magnificently did he display strength of hand and body combined with magnificent horsemanship. Then as if he had got hold of a treasure he rode off with his prisoner to Caesar. Titus congratulated the captor on his amazing strength, and ordered the captive to be executed for his part in the attempt on the wall, then turned his personal attention to the battle for the Temple and the speedier construction of the platforms.

The Jews were suffering so severely in every engagement, as the war slowly but surely approached its culmination and crept nearer to the Sanctuary, that, as if dealing with a diseased body, they cut off the affected limbs to prevent the spread of the infection. They set fire to the section of the north-west colonnade that was joined to Antonia, and then demolished some thirty feet of it, thus beginning the burning down of their holy places with their own hands. Two days later, on the 24th of the last-named month (Panemos), the adjoining colonnade was fired by the Romans. When the flames had advanced over seventy-five feet, the Jews as before cut away the roof, and showing no regard whatever for this masterpiece of architecture, severed the link it provided with Antonia. With this in mind, though they had a chance to stop the lighting of the fire, they did not even lift a finger as the flames approached, and regarded the progress of the fire in the light of their own advantage.

The Fall of Jerusalem

Around the Temple there was no break in the fighting, battle raging continuously between small raiding parties of both sides.

During this period one of the Jews called Jonathan, a man of small stature and nothing much to look at, whose birth and attainments were negligible, stepped forward opposite the tomb of John the High Priest, heaped contempt and abuse on the heads of the Romans, and challenged the bravest of them to single combat. Of the Romans lined up at that point the majority treated him with contempt; some in all probability were frightened, while a few were struck by the very reasonable thought that a man who was looking for death was not one to be engaged at close quarters: those who despaired of their lives might well have uncontrollable passions and the willing help of the Almighty; and to risk everything in a duel with one whose defeat would be nothing to boast of, and whose victory would be disgraceful as well as dangerous, was an act not of courage but of recklessness. For a long time no one came forward and the Jew hurled a volley of gibes at their cowardice, for he had a great admiration for himself and contempt for the Romans. But at last one Pudens, a member of a cavalry squadron, sickened by his arrogant vapourings and no doubt foolishly over-confident because of his small stature, ran out, joined battle, and was getting the better of it when fortune left him in the lurch: he fell, and Jonathan ran up and dispatched him. Then standing on the body he brandished his dripping sword and with his left hand waved his shield, shouting vociferously at the troops, crowing over the fallen man, and mocking

Antonia Captured and Destroyed

the Romans as they watched. At length, while he still jumped about and played the fool, Priscus, a centurion, shot an arrow which pierced him through; at this shouts went up from Jews and Romans – very different in character. Jonathan, spinning round in his agony, fell down on the body of his foe, clear proof that in war undeserved success instantly brings on itself the vengeance of heaven.

The partisans in the Temple never slackened their overt endeavours to cause daily losses to the soldiers working on the platforms, and on the 27th of the same month they devised the following ruse. In the western colonnade they filled the space between the joists and the ceiling below them with dry wood, bitumen, and pitch, then withdrew as if tired out. Thereupon many thoughtless soldiers, carried away by reckless eagerness, charged after those retreating, and erecting ladders ran up to the colonnade. The more sensible men, suspicious of the unexplained Jewish withdrawal, made no move. However, the colonnade was crowded with the men who had climbed on to it, and at that moment the Jews fired it from end to end. As the flames shot up suddenly all round, the Romans who were out of danger were seized with utter consternation, the trapped men with complete helplessness. Encircled by the blaze some flung themselves down into the City behind them, some into the thick of the foe; many in the hope of escaping with their lives jumped down among their own men and broke their legs; most for all their haste were too slow for the fire; a few cheated the flames with their own daggers. Even those destined for a different end were promptly trapped by the wide extension of the conflagration. Caesar, though angry with the victims for having climbed on to the colonnade without orders, was at the same time moved with human compassion; and though no one could hope to rescue them, it was some comfort to the dying men to see the one for whom they were giving their lives so distressed; for as he called out to them, and dashed forward and urged those around him to do everything possible to help them, he could be seen by all. Taking with him those shouts, that sympathy, like a glorious winding-sheet, every man died happy. Some indeed retired to the wide colonnade wall and got clear of the fire, but they were trapped by the Jews, and, after long holding out in spite of their many wounds, finally perished to a man.

Last to fall was a young man named Longus, who added glory to the whole tragic tale and, though every single one of the men who died deserved to be mentioned, outshone them all. Full of admiration for his prowess and in any case unable to get at him, the Jews invited him to come down to them under a pledge of safety; his brother Cornelius, on the other hand, adjured him not to tarnish his own renown and disgrace the Roman army. Convinced that he was right, Longus held up his sword in the sight of the opposing lines and plunged it into his heart. Among those trapped by the flames one Artorius saved his life by a trick. He called to him a fellow-soldier, Lucius, who shared his tent, and yelled: 'I will leave you everything I have if you will come close and catch me.' Lucius eagerly ran to his aid; then Artorius jumped on top of him and survived, but his weight dashed his rescuer to the stone pavement, killing him instantly.

For a time this terrible blow filled the Romans with despondency; but it helped them in the long run by making them more wary and putting them on their guard against Jewish traps, in which they suffered chiefly through ignorance of the ground and through the character of their opponents. The colonnade was burnt down as far as the tower which John in his struggle with Simon had built over the gates opening on to the Gymnasium; the rest, now that the men who had climbed on to it had been wiped out, the Jews cut away. The next day the Romans took a turn, setting light to the entire northern colonnade as far as its junction with the eastern where the angle between the two overhung the Kidron Valley, to which there was a terrifying drop. Here for the present we leave the struggle for the Temple.

In the City famine raged, its victims dropping dead in countless numbers, and the horrors were unspeakable. In every home, if the shadow of something to eat was anywhere detected, war broke out and the best of friends came to grips with each other, snatching away the most wretched means of support. Not even the dying were believed to be in want; at their last gasp they were searched by the bandits in case some of them had food inside their clothes and were feigning death. Open-mouthed with hunger like mad dogs, the desperadoes stumbled and staggered along, hammering at the doors like drunken men, and in their helpless state breaking into the same houses two or three times in a single hour. Necessity made them put their teeth in everything; things which not even the filthiest of dumb animals would look at they picked up and brought themselves to swallow. In the end they actually devoured belts and shoes, and stripped off the leather from their shields and chewed it. Some tried to live on scraps of old hay; for there were people who collected the stalks and sold a tiny bunch for four Attic drachmas!

But why should I speak of the inanimate things that hunger made them shameless enough to eat? I am going now to relate a deed for which there is no parallel in the annals of Greece or any other country, a deed horrible to speak of and incredible to hear. For myself, I am so anxious that future ages should not suspect me of grotesque inventions that I would gladly have passed over this calamity in silence, had there not been countless witnesses of my own generation to bear me out; and besides, my country would have little reason to thank me if I drew a veil over the miseries that were so real to her.

There was a woman, Mary, daughter of Eleazar, who lived east of Jordan in the village of Bethezub ('House of Hyssop'). She was of good family and very rich, and had fled with the rest of the population to Jerusalem, where she shared in the horrors of the siege. Most of the property she had packed up and moved from Peraea into the City had been plundered by the party chiefs; the remnants of her treasures and any food she had managed to obtain were being carried off in daily raids by their henchmen. The wretched woman was filled with uncontrollable fury, and let loose a stream of abuse and curses that enraged the looters against her. When neither re-

Antonia Captured and Destroyed

sentiment nor pity caused anyone to kill her and she grew tired of finding food for others – and whichever way she turned it was almost impossible to find – and while hunger was eating her heart out and rage was consuming her still faster, she yielded to the suggestions of fury and necessity, and in defiance of all natural feeling laid hands on her own child, a baby at the breast. 'Poor little mite!' she cried. 'In war, famine, and civil strife why should I keep you alive? With the Romans there is only slavery, even if we are alive when they come; but famine is forestalling slavery, and the partisans are crueller than either. Come, you must be food for me, to the partisans an avenging spirit, and to the world a tale, the only thing left to fill up the measure of Jewish misery.' As she spoke she killed her son, then roasted him and ate one half, concealing and saving up the rest.

At once the partisans appeared, and sniffing the unholy smell threatened that if she did not produce what she had prepared they would kill her on the spot. She replied that she had kept a fine helping for them, and uncovered what was left of her child. Overcome with instant horror and amazement, they could not take their eyes off the sight. But she went on: 'This child is my own, and the deed is mine too. Help yourselves: I have had my share. Don't be softer than a woman or more tender-hearted than a mother. But if you are squeamish and don't approve of my sacrifice – well, I have eaten half, so you may as well leave me the rest.' That was the last straw, and they went away quivering. They had never before shrunk from anything, and did not much like giving up even this food to the mother. From that moment the

The Fall of Jerusalem

entire city could think of nothing else but this abomination; everyone saw the tragedy before his own eyes and shuddered as if the crime was his. The one desire of the starving was for death; how they envied those who had gone before seeing or hearing of these appalling horrors!

It was not long before the dreadful news reached the Romans. Some of them refused to believe, some were distressed, but on most the effect was to add enormously to their detestation of the Jewish race. Caesar disclaimed all responsibility in the sight of God for this latest tragedy. He had offered the Jews peace and self-government with an amnesty for all offenders; but they had rejected concord in favour of strife, peace in favour of war, plenty and abundance in favour of hunger, and with their own hands had tried to burn down the Temple which the Romans were safeguarding on their behalf; so this food was just what they deserved. Nevertheless he would bury this abomination of infanticide and cannibalism under the ruins of their country, and would not let a city in which mothers fed themselves thus remain on the face of the earth for the sun to look upon. It was even more revolting for mothers to eat such food than for fathers, who even after such appalling tragedies remained in arms. While he made this clear, he was thinking also of the desperation of these men: they would never see reason after enduring all the agonies which they might so easily have avoided by a change of heart.

The Temple Burnt and the City Taken

By now two of the legions had completed their platforms, and on the 8th of Loös Titus ordered the rams to be brought up opposite the western recess of the outer court of the Temple. For six days before they arrived the most powerful battering-ram of all had been pounding the wall incessantly without result: this like the others made no impression on stones so huge and so perfectly bonded. At the northern gate a second team attempted to undermine the foundations, and by tremendous efforts they did lever out the stones in front; but the inner stones supported the weight and the gate stood firm, till despairing of all attempts with engines and crowbars they set up ladders against the colonnades. The Jews were in no hurry to stop them, but when they climbed up they were violently assailed; some were pushed backwards and sent headlong, others clashed with the defenders and were killed; many as they stepped off the ladders were unable to get behind their shields before they were run through with swords, while a few ladders crowded with heavy infantry were pushed sideways at the top and overturned; the Jews too suffered severe losses. Those who had brought up the standards fought hard for them, knowing that it would be a terrible disgrace if they were captured; but in the end the Jews even captured the standards, destroying every man who climbed up. The rest, demoralized by the fate of the fallen, withdrew. On the Roman side not a man died till he had accomplished something; of the partisans all who had distinguished themselves in earlier battles shone once more in this, as did Eleazar, nephew of the party chief Simon. Titus, seeing that his attempts to spare a foreign temple meant injury and death to his soldiers, ordered the gates to be set on fire.

At this time two men deserted Simon, Ananus from Emmaus, the most bloodthirsty of his henchmen, and Archelaus, son of Magaddatus, expecting a free pardon as they were quitting the Jews when they were getting the better of it. Denouncing this as another of their dirty tricks and aware of their habitual cruelty to their own people, Titus was strongly inclined to kill them both, pointing out that they had been forced to it by necessity and had not come by free choice, and that men did not deserve to live if they first set their own city on fire and then jumped clear. However, anger could not stand against his own pledged word and he let the men go, though he did not grant them the same privileges as the others.

By now the soldiers were setting fire to the gates. The silver melted and ran, quickly exposing the woodwork to the flames, which were carried from there in a solid wall and fastened on to the colonnades. When the Jews saw the ring of fire, they lost all power of body and mind; such was their consternation that not a finger was raised to keep out or quench the flames; they stood looking on in utter helplessness. Yet their dismay at the present destruction made them no wiser for the future, but as if the Sanctuary itself was already in flames they whipped up their rage against the Romans. All that day and the following night the flames were in possession: the colonnades could not be fired all at once but only bit by bit.

The next day Titus ordered a section of his army to put out the fire, and to make a road close to the gates to facilitate the approach of the legions. Then he summoned a council of war, attended by the six senior generals – Tiberius Alexander, the camp prefect; Sextus Cerealis, Larcius Lepidus, and Titus Phrygius, commanding the Fifth, Tenth, and Fifteenth Legions respectively; Aeternius Fronto, tribune in charge of the two legions from Alexandria; and Marcus Antonius Julianus, procurator of Judaea. After these the other procurators and tribunes were brought in, and Titus invited opinions on the question of the Sanctuary. Some insisted that they should enforce the law of war: there would be continual revolts while the Sanctuary remained as a rallying-point for Jews all over the world. Others argued that if the Jews evacuated it and no armed man was allowed on it, it should be spared, but if they climbed on it for military purposes it should be burnt down; it would in that case be a fortress, not a sanctuary, and from then on the impiety would be blameable not on the Romans but on those who forced their hands. Titus replied that even if the Jews did climb on it for military purposes, he would not make war on inanimate objects instead of men, or, whatever happened, burn down such a work of art: it was the Romans who would lose thereby, just as their empire would gain an ornament if it was preserved.

The Fall of Jerusalem

Fronto, Alexander, and Cerealis now confidently came over to this opinion. Titus thereupon adjourned the meeting, and instructing the officers to give the remainder of the army time for rest, so that he should find them full of new vigour when fighting was resumed, he ordered the picked men of all the cohorts to make a road through the ruins and put out the fire.

All that day exhaustion and consternation subdued the enterprise of the Jews; but on the next, having recovered both strength and confidence, they made a sortie through the East Gate against the garrison of the outer court of the Temple at about 8 a.m. Their onslaught met with stubborn resistance from the Romans, who sheltered behind a wall of steel and closed their ranks, though it was obvious that they could not hold together long, as the raiding party surpassed them in numbers and determination. Anticipating the collapse of the line Caesar, who was watching from Antonia, came to the rescue with his picked horsemen. The Jews broke before their onset, and when the front-rank men fell the rest withdrew. But whenever the Romans gave ground they whipped round and pressed them hard: when the Romans turned about they retreated again, till at about 11 o'clock they were overpowered and shut up in the inner court.

Titus retired to Antonia, intending to launch a full-scale attack at dawn the next day and surround the Sanctuary completely. It had, however, been condemned to the flames by God long ago: by the turning of time's wheel the fated day had now come, the 10th of Loös, the day which centuries before had seen it burnt by the king

The Temple Burnt and the City Taken

of Babylon. But it was the Jews themselves who caused and started this conflagration. When Titus had retired, the partisans remained quiet for a time, then again attacked the Romans, the garrison of the Sanctuary clashing with those who were putting out the fire in the inner court, and who routed the Jews and chased them as far as the Sanctuary. Then one of the soldiers, without waiting for orders and without a qualm for the terrible consequences of his action but urged on by some unseen force, snatched up a blazing piece of wood and climbing on another soldier's back hurled the brand through a golden aperture giving access on the north side to the chambers built round the Sanctuary. As the flames shot into the air the Jews sent up a cry that matched the calamity and dashed to the rescue, with no thought now of saving their lives or husbanding their strength; for that which hitherto they had guarded so devotedly was disappearing before their eyes.

A runner brought the news to Titus as he was resting in his tent after the battle. He leapt up as he was and ran to the Sanctuary to extinguish the blaze. His whole staff panted after him, followed by the excited legions with all the shouting and confusion inseparable from the disorganized rush of an immense army. Caesar shouted and waved to the combatants to put out the fire; but his shouts were unheard as their ears were deafened by a greater din, and his gesticulations went unheeded amidst the distractions of battle and bloodshed. As the legions charged in, neither persuasion nor threat could check their impetuosity: passion alone was in command. Crowded together round the entrances many were trampled by their friends, many fell among the still hot and smoking ruins of the colonnades and died as miserably as the defeated. As they neared the Sanctuary they pretended not even to hear Caesar's commands and urged the men in front to throw in more firebrands. The partisans were no longer in a position to help; everywhere was slaughter and flight. Most of the victims were peaceful citizens, weak and unarmed, butchered wherever they were caught. Round the Altar the heap of corpses grew higher and higher, while down the Sanctuary steps poured a river of blood and the bodies of those killed at the top slithered to the bottom. The soldiers were like men possessed and there was no holding them, nor was there any arguing with the fire. Caesar therefore led his staff inside the building and viewed the Holy Place of the Sanctuary with its furnishings, which went far beyond the accounts circulating in foreign countries, and fully justified their splendid reputation in our own. The flames were not yet effecting an entry from any direction but were feeding on the chambers built round the Sanctuary; so realizing that there was still time to save the glorious edifice, Titus dashed out and by personal efforts strove to persuade his men to put out the fire, instructing Liberalius, a centurion of his bodyguard of spearmen, to lay his staff across the shoulders of any who disobeyed. But their respect for Caesar and their fear of the centurion's staff were powerless against their fury, their detestation of the Jews, and an uncontrollable lust for battle. Most of them were also spurred on by the expectation of loot, being convinced that the interior was bursting with money and seeing that everything outside was of gold. But they were forestalled by one of those who had gone in. When Caesar dashed out to restrain the troops, that man pushed a firebrand into the hinges of the gate. Then from within a flame suddenly shot up, Caesar and his staff withdrew, and those outside were free to start what fires they liked. Thus the Sanctuary was set on fire in defiance of Caesar's wishes.

Grief might well be bitter for the destruction of the most wonderful edifice ever seen or heard of, both for its size and construction and for the lavish perfection of detail and the glory of its holy places; yet we find very real comfort in the thought that Fate is inexorable, not only towards living beings but also towards buildings and sites. We may wonder too at the exactness of the cycle of Fate: she kept, as I said, to the very month and day which centuries before had seen the Sanctuary burnt by the Babylonians. From its first foundation by King Solomon to its present destruction, which occurred in the second year of Vespasian's reign, was a period of 1,130 years, 7 months and 15 days; from its rebuilding in the second year of King Cyrus, for which Haggai was responsible, to its capture under Vespasian was 639 years and 45 days.

While the Sanctuary was burning, looting went on right and left and all who were caught were put to the sword. There was no pity for age, no regard for rank; little children and old men, laymen and priests alike were butchered; every class was held in the iron embrace of war, whether they defended themselves or cried for mercy. Through the roar of the flames as they swept relentlessly on could be heard the groans of the falling:

such were the height of the hill and the vastness of the blazing edifice that the entire city seemed to be on fire, while as for the noise, nothing could be imagined more shattering or more horrifying. There was the war-cry of the Roman legions as they converged; the yells of the partisans encircled with fire and sword; the panic flight of the people cut off above into the arms of the enemy, and their shrieks as the end approached. The cries from the hill were answered from the crowded streets; and now many who were wasted with hunger and beyond speech found strength to moan and wail when they saw the Sanctuary in flames. Back from Peraea and the mountains round about came the echo in a thunderous bass.

Yet more terrible than the din were the sights that met the eye. The Temple Hill, enveloped in flames from top to bottom, appeared to be boiling up from its very roots; yet the sea of flame was nothing to the ocean of blood, or the companies of killers to the armies of killed: nowhere could the ground be seen between the corpses, and the soldiers climbed over heaps of bodies as they chased the fugitives. The terrorist horde pushed the Romans back, and by a violent struggle burst through into the outer court of the Temple and from there into the City, the few surviving members of the public taking refuge on the outer colonnade. Some of the priests at first tore up from the Sanctuary the spikes with their lead sockets and threw them at the Romans. Then as they were no better off and the flames were leaping towards them, they retired to the wall, which was twelve feet wide, and stayed there. However, two men of note,

The Temple Burnt and the City Taken

in a position either to save their lives by going over to the Romans or to face with the others whatever came their way, threw themselves into the fire and were burnt to ashes with the Sanctuary – Meirus, son of Belgas, and Joseph, son of Dalaeus.

The Romans, judging it useless to spare the outbuildings now that the Sanctuary was in flames, set fire to them all – what remained of the colonnades and all the gates except two, one on the east end, the other on the south, both of which they later demolished. They also burnt the treasuries which housed huge sums of money, huge quantities of clothing, and other precious things; here, in fact, all the wealth of the Jews was piled up, for the rich had dismantled their houses and brought the contents here for safe keeping. Next they came to the last surviving colonnade of the outer court. On this women and children and a mixed crowd of citizens had found a refuge – 6,000 in all. Before Caesar could reach a decision about them or instruct his officers, the soldiers, carried away by their fury, fired the colonnade from below; as a result some flung themselves out of the flames to their death, others perished in the blaze: of that vast number there escaped not one. Their destruction was due to a false prophet who that very day had declared to the people in the City that God commanded them to go up into the Temple to receive the signs of their deliverance. A number of hireling prophets had been put up in recent days by the party chiefs to deceive the people by exhorting them to await help from God, and so to reduce the number of deserters and buoy up with hope those who were above fear and anxiety. Man

The Fall of Jerusalem

is readily persuaded in adversity: when the deceiver actually promises deliverance from the miseries that envelop him, then the sufferer becomes the willing slave of hope. So it was that the unhappy people were beguiled at that stage by cheats and false messengers of God, while the unmistakable portents that foreshadowed the coming desolation they treated with indifference and incredulity, disregarding God's warnings as if they were moonstruck, blind and senseless. First a star stood over the City, very like a broadsword, and a comet that remained a whole year. Then before the revolt and the movement to war, while the people were assembling for the Feast of Unleavened Bread, on the 8th of Xanthicos at 3 a.m. so bright a light shone round the Altar and the Sanctuary that it might have been midday. This lasted half an hour. The inexperienced took it for a good omen, but the sacred scribes at once gave an interpretation which the event proved right. During the same feast a cow brought by someone to be sacrificed gave birth to a lamb in the middle of the Temple courts, while at midnight it was observed that the East Gate of the inner court had opened of its own accord – a gate made of bronze and so solid that every evening twenty strong men were required to shut it; it was fastened with iron-bound bars and secured by bolts which were lowered a long way into a threshold fashioned from a single slab of stone. The temple-guards ran with the news to the Captain, who came up and by a great effort managed to shut it. This like the other seemed to the laity to be the best of omens: had not God opened to them the gate of happiness? But the learned perceived that the security of the Sanctuary was dissolving of its own accord, and that the opening of the gate was a gift to the enemy; and they admitted in their hearts that the sign was a portent of desolation.

A few days after the Feast, on the 21st of Artemisios, a supernatural apparition was seen, too amazing to be believed. What I have to relate would, I suppose, have been dismissed as an invention, had it not been vouched for by eyewitnesses and followed by disasters that bore out the signs. Before sunset there were seen in the sky, over the whole country, chariots and regiments in arms speeding through the clouds and encircling the towns. Again, at the Feast of Pentecost, when the priests had gone into the inner court of the Temple at night to perform the usual ceremonies, they declared that they were aware, first of a violent movement and a loud crash, then of a concerted cry: 'Let us go hence.'

An incident more alarming still had occurred four years before the war at a time of exceptional peace and prosperity for the City. One Jeshua, son of Ananias, a very ordinary yokel, came to the feast at which every Jew is expected to set up a tabernacle for God. As he stood in the Temple he suddenly began to shout: 'A voice from the east, a voice from the west, a voice from the four winds, a voice against Jerusalem and the Sanctuary, a voice against bridegrooms and brides, a voice against the whole people.' Day and night he uttered this cry as he went through all the streets. Some of the more prominent citizens, very annoyed at these ominous words, laid hold of the fellow and beat him savagely. Without saying a word in his own defence or for the private information of his persecutors, he persisted in shouting the same warning as before. The Jewish authorities, rightly concluding that some supernatural force was responsible for the man's behaviour, took him before the Roman procurator. There, though scourged till his flesh hung in ribbons, he neither begged for mercy nor shed a tear, but lowering his voice to the most mournful of tones answered every blow with 'Woe to Jerusalem!' When Albinus – for that was the procurator's name – demanded to know who he was, where he came from and why he uttered such cries, he made no reply whatever to the questions but endlessly repeated his lament over the City, till Albinus decided that he was a madman and released him. All the time till the war broke out he never approached another citizen or was seen in conversation, but daily as if he had learnt a prayer by heart he recited his lament: 'Woe to Jerusalem!' Those who daily cursed him he never cursed; those who gave him food he never thanked: his only response to anyone was that dismal foreboding. His voice was heard most of all at the feasts. For seven years and five months he went on ceaselessly, his voice as strong as ever and his vigour unabated, till during the siege after seeing the fulfilment of his foreboding he was silenced. He was going round on the wall uttering his piercing cry: 'Woe again to the City, the people, and the Sanctuary!' and as he added a last word: 'Woe to me also!' a stone shot from an engine struck him, killing him instantly. Thus he uttered those same forebodings to the very end.

Anyone who ponders these things will find that God cares for mankind and in all possible ways foreshows to

The Temple Burnt and the City Taken

His people the means of salvation, and that it is through folly and evils of their own choosing that they come to destruction. Thus the Jews after pulling down Antonia made the Temple square, in spite of the warning in their prophetic books that when the Temple became a square the City and Sanctuary would fall. But their chief inducement to go to war was an equivocal oracle also found in their sacred writings, announcing that at that time a man from their country would become monarch of the whole world. This they took to mean the triumph of their own race, and many of their scholars were wildly out in their interpretation. In fact the oracle pointed to the accession of Vespasian; for it was in Judaea he was proclaimed emperor. But it is not possible for men to escape from fate even if they see it coming. The Jews interpreted some of the prophecies to suit themselves and laughed the others off, till by the fall of their city and their own destruction their folly stood revealed.

As the partisans had fled into the City, and flames were consuming the Sanctuary itself and all its surroundings, the Romans brought their standards into the Temple area, and erecting them opposite the East Gate sacrificed to them there, and with thunderous acclamations hailed Titus as *Imperator*. So laden with plunder was every single soldier that all over Syria the value of gold was reduced by half. With the priests holding out on the Sanctuary wall was a lad parched with thirst. He begged the Roman guards to give him safe conduct, openly admitting his thirst. They felt sorry that a mere child should be suffering so, and granted the safe conduct. He came down, drank what he needed, filled the vessel he had brought with water, and dashed off full speed to his friends aloft. He was far too quick for the guards, who swore at him for breaking his word; but he retorted that he had done no such thing, for the agreement had not been that he should stay with them, but only that he should come down and get some water. That was exactly what he had done, so how had he broken his word? Such sharp practice in one so young astounded the victims of his trickery. However, after four days the starving priests came down and were taken by the guards to Titus, whom they begged to spare their lives. He replied that the time for pardon was past, that the one thing that would have justified their being spared had gone, and that the duty of priests was to perish with their sanctuary. Then he pronounced sentence of death.

The partisans and their chiefs, beaten in the war on all sides and shut in by a wall that left them no possibility of escape, invited Titus to a parley. Such was his natural kindness that he was eager to save the town, and urged by his friends, who concluded that the terrorists had at last come to their senses, he took his stand on the west side of the outer court of the Temple; for here above the Gymnasium there were gates, and a bridge linked the Temple with the Upper City; this now separated the party chiefs from Caesar. On either side stood a dense crowd – Jews round Simon and John on tiptoe with hope of pardon, Romans eager to see how Titus would receive their appeal. Titus called on his men to control their fury and their weapons, and placing his interpreter by his side exercised the victor's privilege and spoke first.

'Are you satisfied now, gentlemen, with the sufferings

The Temple Burnt and the City Taken

of your country? you who, in utter disregard of our strength and your weakness, have through your reckless impetuosity and madness destroyed your people, your city, and your Sanctuary, and richly deserve the destruction that is coming to yourselves; you who from the moment Pompey's forces crushed you have never stopped rebelling, and now have made open war on Rome. Did you rely on numbers? Why, a tiny fraction of the Roman army sufficed to deal with you! Well then; on the trustworthiness of your allies? And which of the nations outside our empire was going to prefer Jews to Romans? Or on your wonderful physique? Yet you know that the Germans are our slaves. On the strength of your walls? What wall could be a better obstacle than the open sea that is the bulwark of Britain? But Britain was brought to her knees by the arms of Rome! On your invincible determination and the wiles of your generals? Yet you know that even Carthage was overwhelmed!

'There is only one answer. You were incited against the Romans by Roman kindness. First we gave you the land to occupy and set over you kings of your own race; then we upheld the laws of your fathers, and allowed you complete control of your internal and external affairs; above all, we permitted you to raise taxes for God and to collect offerings, and we neither discouraged nor interfered with those who brought them – so that you could grow richer to our detriment and prepare at our expense to make war on us! Then, enjoying such advantages, you flung your abundance at the heads of those who furnished it, and like beasts you bit the hand that fed you!

The Fall of Jerusalem

'No doubt you despised Nero for his idleness, and like lesions or sprains you remained quiescent but malignant for a time, and then, when a more serious illness broke out, you came out into the open and let your limitless ambitions grow into insolent presumption. My father came into the country, not to punish you for what you did in Cestius' time, but to caution you. If he had come to put an end to the nation, the right thing would have been to go straight to the root of your strength and sack this city at once. In actual fact he ravaged Galilee and the outlying districts, giving you time to come to your senses. But you took generosity for weakness, and our gentleness only served to increase your audacity. When Nero died you sank to the lowest level of depravity and took advantage of our difficulties at home: when my father and I had gone away to Egypt, you jumped at the chance to prepare for war, and you shamelessly created difficulties once we were emperors, though when we were generals you had found us so considerate. When the whole Empire had come to us for protection, when all its inhabitants were enjoying the blessings of peace and countries outside were sending embassies to congratulate us, once again the Jews rose against us. You sent embassies beyond the Euphrates to stir up a revolt; you rebuilt your city walls; there were faction-fights, rival party chiefs, civil war – just what we should expect from men so depraved!

'I came to the city bearing sombre injunctions which it had pained my father to give. When I heard that the citizens were peacefully inclined, I was delighted. You others I begged to desist before hostilities began; long

The Temple Burnt and the City Taken

after you had begun them I spared you, giving safe conduct to deserters and keeping faith with them when they came to me for protection. For many prisoners I showed pity: the warmongers I punished with torture and death. Most unwillingly I brought engines to bear on your walls: my soldiers, ever thirsting for your blood, I held in leash: after every victory, as if it was a defeat, I appealed to you for an armistice. When I got near to the Temple, I again deliberately forwent my rights as victor and appealed to you to spare your own holy places and preserve the Sanctuary for your own use, offering you freedom to come out and a guarantee of safety or, if you wished, a chance to fight on other ground. Every proposal you treated with scorn, and your Sanctuary you set on fire with your own hands!

'After all that, you disgusting people, do you now invite me to a conference? What have you to save that can be compared with what has gone? What security do you think you deserve after the loss of your Sanctuary? Why, even now you stand in arms, and not even at your last gasp so much as pretend to be asking for mercy. You poor fools, what are you pinning your faith on? Aren't your people dead, your Sanctuary gone, your city in my power, your very lives in my hands? Do you think you will win renown for your courage by putting off death till the last moment? *I* shall not compete with you in craziness. If you throw down your arms and surrender your persons, I will grant you your lives; like an easy-going head of a house, I will punish what cannot be cured and spare the rest for my own use.'

To this they replied that they could accept no terms

from him as they had sworn never to do so; but they asked leave to go out through the circumvallation with their wives and children, in which case they would go away into the desert and leave the City to him. Titus, furious that men no better than prisoners should put forward demands as if they had defeated him, ordered it to be announced that it was no longer any use their deserting or hoping for terms, as he would spare no one: they must fight to the last ditch and save themselves in any way they could; from now on he would insist on all his rights as victor. Then he gave his men leave to burn and sack the City. They did nothing that day, but on the next they fired the Muniment Office, the Citadel, the Council Chamber, and the area known as Ophel. The fire spread as far as Helena's Palace in the centre of the Citadel, consuming the narrow streets and the houses full of the bodies of those who had died of starvation.

On the same day King Izates' sons and brothers, joined by many prominent citizens, besought Caesar to grant them protection. Though furious with all the survivors, he lived up to his character and received the applicants. For the time being he kept them all in custody; the king's sons and kinsmen he put in chains and later conveyed to Rome to serve as hostages.

The partisans made a rush towards the Palace, which was so solidly built that many had stored their property there. They drove away the Romans, slaughtered the people who had crowded into the building, 8,400 in number, and looted the riches. They also took two of the Romans alive, a cavalryman and an infantryman. The infantryman they butchered then and there and dragged round the City, as if by proxy they were revenging themselves on all the Romans. As the cavalryman said that he had something to suggest that might save their lives, he was taken into Simon's presence; but when he got there he had nothing to say, so was handed over to Ardalas, one of the officers, to be executed. Ardalas tied his hands behind him and blindfolded him, then marched him forward in full view of the Romans with the intention of cutting off his head; but by a sudden movement the man dashed away to the Roman lines just as the Jew drew his sword. As he had made his escape from the enemy Titus could not very well put him to death, but deciding that he was unfit to be a soldier of Rome as he had let himself be taken alive, he stripped him of his arms and expelled him from the legion, to a man with any self-respect a punishment worse than death.

Next day the Romans drove the terrorists from the Lower City and burnt the whole place as far as Siloam. They were glad enough to see the town destroyed but got precious little loot, as the whole area had been cleaned out by the partisans before they withdrew to the Upper City. These men felt no remorse for the mischief they had done – they boasted as if they were proud of it: when they saw the City burning, they laughed heartily and said they were happily awaiting the end; for, with the people slaughtered, the Sanctuary burnt to the ground, and the town blazing, they were leaving nothing to the enemy. Yet to the very last Josephus never wearied of appealing to them to spare what was left of the City, though however much he might say against their

The Fall of Jerusalem

savagery and impiety, however much advice he might give them for their own good, he got nothing but ridicule in return. As they could not very well surrender because of their oath and were unable now to fight the Romans on equal terms, they were like caged animals, so used to killing that they thirsted for blood. They scattered through the outskirts of the City and lay in wait among the ruins for would-be deserters. Many in fact were caught, and as hunger had left them too weak even to run away, all were butchered and their bodies thrown to the dogs. But any kind of death was more bearable than starvation, so that although they had no hope now of mercy from the Romans, they still fled to them, falling into the murderous hands of the partisans with their eyes open. Not one spot in the whole City was empty: every single one had its corpse, the victim of hunger or faction.

The last hope that bolstered up the party chiefs and their terrorist gangs lay in the underground sewers. If they took refuge in them they did not expect to be tracked down, and their intention was to come out and make good their escape after the final capture of the City and the subsequent departure of the Romans. But this was only an idle dream: they were not fated to escape from either God or the Romans. At the time, however, they had such faith in their bolt-holes that they lit more fires than did the Romans. Those who fled from the burning buildings into the sewers they killed without hesitation and plundered; if they found anyone with food they snatched it away and swallowed it, dripping with the wretched man's blood. By now they were actually fighting each other for the loot; and I have little doubt that if capture had not forestalled it, their utter bestiality would have made them get their teeth into the very corpses.

Owing to the steep approach on every side it was not feasible to master the Upper City without platforms, so on the 20th of Loös Caesar divided up the work among the troops. It was difficult to transport the timber since, as mentioned before, all the neighbourhood for over eleven miles had been stripped bare for the earlier platforms. The four legions raised their earthworks on the west side of the City opposite the Palace, while the whole body of allies and the rest of the army worked near the Gymnasium, the bridge and Simon's tower, built during the struggle with John as a stronghold for himself.

At this time the Idumaean chiefs at a secret meeting discussed the question of piecemeal surrender, and sent five men to Titus to implore his protection. Hoping that the party chiefs too would give in if they lost the support of the Idumaeans who had made so large a contribution to the war, Titus hesitated at first, but finally granted them their lives and sent the men back. But as they got ready to go, Simon saw what was afoot, immediately put to death the five who had gone to Titus, seized the chiefs of whom the most prominent was Jacob, son of Sosas, and threw them into prison. On the Idumaean rank and file, at a loss without their leaders, he kept a careful eye, posting more efficient sentry-groups along the wall. However, the sentries were unable to cope with the deserters: though many were killed, far more got away. The Romans received them all, Titus through kindness of heart disregarding his earlier proclamation, and the men holding their hands because they were sick of killing and hopeful of gain. For only the townsmen were kept back – all the rest were sold along with the women and children, the retail price being very low, as supply was far in excess of demand. In spite of his earlier announcement that no one must desert alone, but must bring his family with him, he nevertheless received such people; but he appointed officers to separate from them anyone deserving punishment. The number sold was enormous: the number of townsmen spared was over 40,000; these were free to go wherever they thought fit.

During this same period a priest named Jeshua, son of Thebuthi, obtained from Caesar a sworn guarantee of safety on condition that he should hand over some of the sacred treasures. He came out and handed over from the Sanctuary wall two lampstands closely resembling those kept in the Sanctuary, as well as tables, basins, and cups, all of solid gold and very heavy. He also handed over the curtains, the vestments of the high priests with the precious stones, and many other articles required for the Temple services. In addition the Temple treasurer Phineas, when taken prisoner, produced the tunics and girdles of the priests and a large supply of purple and scarlet kept in store for repairing the great curtain, together with cinnamon in bulk, cassia, and quantities of other spices, which were blended and daily burnt as incense to God. He handed over many of the other treasures too, with Temple ornaments in abundance, thus earning though a prisoner the pardon granted to deserters.

In eighteen days the platforms were ready for use, and

on the 7th of Gorpiaios the Romans brought up their engines. Some of the partisans, already despairing of the City, withdrew from the wall to the Citadel, while others plunged into the sewers; but many ranged themselves along the ramparts and tried to repulse the crews of the battering-rams. These too the Romans overwhelmed by numbers and by force, and above all by confidence in face of despondency and half-heartedness. When a section of the wall was broken through and some of the towers gave way before the assault of the rams, there was an immediate flight from the battlements, and even the party chiefs were filled with terror unjustified by the situation: before the enemy got through, they were stunned and ready to fly, and men once arrogant and bragging about their ungodly deeds could now be seen abject and trembling, insomuch that even in these vile scoundrels it was pitiful to note the change. Their one desire was to dash for the wall that shut them in, repulse the guards and hack their way through to safety; but when their old faithful supporters were nowhere to be seen – they had been forced to scatter in all directions – and when runners announced that the whole west wall was down, or that the Romans had broken in and were just round the corner seeking them, while others blinded by terror declared that from the towers they could actually see the enemy, they fell on their faces bewailing their own insane folly, and as if hamstrung were incapable of flight.

What happened would serve as an object-lesson, showing both the power of God over the wicked and the luck of the Romans. For the party chiefs divested themselves of their safety, and of their own accord came down from the towers on which they could never have been subdued by force but only by starvation; and the Romans, who had toiled so hard to break through the weaker walls, captured by sheer luck those which their engines could not touch; for no mechanical device could have made any impression on the three towers described elsewhere. Abandoning these, or rather driven down from them by God, they took refuge for a moment in the ravine below Siloam; later, when they had recovered somewhat from their terror, they made a dash for the nearest section of the circumvallation. But their strength was broken now by terror and disaster, and their courage could not rise to the occasion; so they were repulsed by the guards, scattered this way and that, and plunged into the sewers.

Masters now of the walls, the Romans set up their standards on the towers and with clapping and singing celebrated their victory, having found the end of the war much easier than the beginning. They had surmounted the last wall without losing a man – it seemed too good to be true – and when they found no one to oppose them, they could make nothing of it. They poured into the streets sword in hand, cut down without mercy all who came within reach, and burnt the houses of any who took refuge indoors, occupants and all. Many they raided, and as they entered in search of plunder, they found whole families dead and the rooms full of the victims of starvation: horrified by the sight, they emerged empty-handed. Pity for those who had died in this way was matched by no such feeling for the living: they ran every man through whom they met and blocked the narrow streets with corpses, deluging the whole City with gore so that many of the fires were quenched by the blood of the slain. At dusk the slaughter ceased, but in the night the fire gained the mastery, and on the 8th of Gorpiaios the sun rose over Jerusalem in flames – a city that during the siege had suffered such disasters that if she had enjoyed as many blessings from her foundation, she would have been the envy of the world, and a city that deserved these terrible misfortunes on no other account than that she produced a generation such as brought about her ruin.

When Titus entered he was astounded by the strength of the city, and especially by the towers which the party chiefs in their mad folly had abandoned. Observing how solid they were all the way up, how huge each block of stone and how accurately fitted, how great their breadth and how immense their height, he exclaimed aloud: 'God has been on our side; it is God who brought the Jews down from these strongholds; for what could human hands or instruments do against such towers?' At that time he made many such remarks to his friends, and he set free all persons imprisoned by the party chiefs and found in the forts. Later, when he destroyed the rest of the City and pulled down the walls, he left the towers as a monument to his own luck, which had proved his ally and enabled him to overcome impregnable defences.

As the soldiers were now growing weary of bloodshed and survivors were still appearing in large numbers, Caesar gave orders that only men who offered armed resistance were to be killed, and everyone else taken alive. But as well as those covered by the orders the aged and infirm were slaughtered: men in their prime who might be useful were herded into the Temple and shut up in the Court of the Women. To guard them Caesar appointed one of his freedmen, and his friend Fronto to decide each man's fate according to his deserts. Those who had taken part in sedition and terrorism informed against each other, and Fronto executed the lot. Of the youngsters he picked out the tallest and handsomest to be kept for the triumphal procession; of the rest, those over seventeen were put in irons and sent to hard labour in Egypt, while great numbers were presented by Titus to the provinces to perish in the theatres by the sword or by wild beasts; those under seventeen were sold. During the days in which Fronto was sorting them out starvation killed 11,000 of the prisoners, some because the guards hated them too bitterly to allow them any food, others because they would not accept it when offered; in any case there was not even enough corn to fill so many mouths.

All the prisoners taken from beginning to end of the war totalled 97,000; those who perished in the long siege 1,100,000. Of these the majority were Jews by race but not Jerusalem citizens: they had come together from the whole country for the Feast of Unleavened Bread and had suddenly been caught up in the war, so that first the overcrowding meant death by pestilence, and later hunger took a heavier toll. That so many could crowd into the City was shown by the census held in Cestius' time. Wishing to bring home the strength of the city to Nero, who despised the nation, Cestius instructed the

The Temple Burnt and the City Taken

chief priests to hold a census of the population, if it was possible to do so. They chose the time of the Passover Feast, at which sacrifice is offered from 3 to 5 p.m., and as it is not permissible to feast alone, a sort of fraternal group is formed round each victim, consisting of at least ten adult males, while many groups have twenty members. The count showed that there were 255,600 victims; the men, reckoning ten diners to each victim, totalled 2,700,000, all ceremonially clean; for persons suffering from leprosy, venereal disease, monthly periods, or any form of defilement were debarred from participation, as were the foreigners who came from abroad in large numbers to be present at the ceremonies.

But now fate had decreed that one prison should confine the whole nation and that a city solid with men should be held fast in war's embrace. No destruction ever wrought by God or man approached the wholesale carnage of this war. Every man who showed himself was either killed or captured by the Romans, and then those in the sewers were ferreted out, the ground was torn up, and all who were trapped were killed. There too were found the bodies of more than 2,000, some killed by their own hand, some by one another's, but most by starvation. So foul a stench of human flesh greeted those who charged in that many turned back at once. Others were so avaricious that they pushed on, climbing over the piles of corpses; for many valuables were found in the passages and all scruples were silenced by the prospect of gain. Many prisoners of the party chiefs were brought up; for not even at their last gasp had they abandoned their brutality. But God rewarded them both as they deserved: John, starving to death with his brothers in the sewers, after many scornful refusals at last appealed to the Romans for mercy, while Simon after battling long against the inevitable, as will be described later, gave himself up. John was sentenced to life-imprisonment, but Simon was kept for the triumphal procession and ultimate execution. The Romans now fired the outlying districts of the town and demolished the walls.

So fell Jerusalem in the second year of Vespasian's reign, on the 8th of Gorpiaios, captured five times before and now for the second time utterly laid waste. Shishak king of Egypt, followed by Antiochus, then Pompey, and after that Sosius and Herod together, captured the City but spared it. Earlier on the king of Babylon had stormed it and laid it waste 1,468 years and 6 months from its foundation. It was originally founded by a Canaanite chieftain called in the vernacular 'King of Righteousness', for such he was. On that account he was the first priest of God and the first to build the Temple and in its honour to give the name of Jerusalem to the City, previously called Salem. The Canaanite inhabitants were driven out by the Jewish king David, who settled his own people there; then 477 years and 6 months after his time it was utterly destroyed by the Babylonians. From King David, the first Jew to reign in it, to the destruction by Titus was 1,179 years. But neither its long history, nor its vast wealth, nor its people dispersed through the whole world, nor the unparalleled renown of its worship sufficed to avert its ruin. So ended the siege of Jerusalem.